MznLnx

Missing Links Exam Preps

Exam Prep for

Brief Calculus: An Applied Approach

Larson And Edwards, 6th Edition

The MznLnx Exam Prep is your link from the texbook and lecture to your exams.
The MznLnx Exam Preps are unauthorized and comprehensive reviews of your textbooks.

All material provided by MznLnx and Rico Publications (c) 2010
Textbook publishers and textbook authors do not particpate in or contribute to these reviews.

MznLnx

Rico Publications

Exam Prep for Brief Calculus: An Applied Approach
6th Edition
Larson And Edwards

Publisher: Raymond Houge
Assistant Editor: Michael Rouger
Text and Cover Designer: Lisa Buckner
Marketing Manager: Sara Swagger
Project Manager, Editorial Production: Jerry Emerson
Art Director: Vernon Lowerui

Product Manager: Dave Mason
Editorial Assitant: Rachel Guzmanji
Pedagogy: Debra Long
Cover Image: Jim Reed/Getty Images
Text and Cover Printer: City Printing, Inc.
Compositor: Media Mix, Inc.

(c) 2010 Rico Publications

ALL RIGHTS RESERVED. No part of this work covered by the copyright may be reproduced or used in any form or by an means--graphic, electronic, or mechanical, including photocopying, recording, taping, Web distribution, information storage, and retrieval systems, or in any other manner--without the written permission of the publisher.

Printed in the United States
ISBN:

For more information about our products, contact us at:

Dave.Mason@RicoPublications.com

For permission to use material from this text or

product, submit a request online to:

Dave.Mason@RicoPublications.com

Contents

CHAPTER 1
A Precalculus Review — 1

CHAPTER 2
Functions, Graphs, and Limits — 13

CHAPTER 3
Differentiation — 33

CHAPTER 4
Applications of the Derivative — 52

CHAPTER 5
Exponential and Logarithmic Functions — 69

CHAPTER 6
Integration and Its Applications — 85

CHAPTER 7
Techniques of Integration — 101

CHAPTER 8
Functions of Several Variables — 116

ANSWER KEY — 135

TO THE STUDENT

COMPREHENSIVE

The *MznLnx* Exam Prep series is designed to help you pass your exams. Editors at MznLnx review your textbooks and then prepare these practice exams to help you master the textbook material. Unlike study guides, workbooks, and practice tests provided by the texbook publisher and textbook authors, *MznLnx* gives you **all** of the material in each chapter in exam form, not just samples, so you can be sure to nail your exam.

MECHANICAL

The MznLnx Exam Prep series creates exams that will help you learn the subject matter as well as test you on your understanding. Each question is designed to help you master the concept. Just working through the exams, you gain an understanding of the subject--its a simple mechanical process that produces success.

INTEGRATED STUDY GUIDE AND REVIEW

MznLnx is not just a set of exams designed to test you, its also a comprehensive review of the subject content. Each exam question is also a review of the concept, making sure that you will get the answer correct without having to go to other sources of material. You learn as you go! Its the easiest way to pass an exam.

HUMOR

Studying can be tedious and dry. MznLnx's instructional design includes moderate humor within the exam questions on occassion, to break the tedium and revitalize the brain

Chapter 1. A Precalculus Review 1

1. Initial objects are also called _____, and terminal objects are also called final.
   a. Thing
   b. Coterminal0
   c. Undefined
   d. Undefined

2. In mathematics, a _____ may be described informally as a number that can be given by an infinite decimal representation.
   a. Thing
   b. Real number0
   c. Undefined
   d. Undefined

3. In mathematics, an _____ is a statement about the relative size or order of two objects.
   a. Thing
   b. Inequality0
   c. Undefined
   d. Undefined

4. A _____ is a set of numbers that designate location in a given reference system, such as x,y in a planar _____ system or an x,y,z in a three-dimensional _____ system.
   a. Coordinate0
   b. Thing
   c. Undefined
   d. Undefined

5. In mathematics, the _____ of a coordinate system is the point where the axes of the system intersect.
   a. Thing
   b. Origin0
   c. Undefined
   d. Undefined

6. The _____ integers are all the integers from zero on upwards.
   a. Nonnegative0
   b. Thing
   c. Undefined
   d. Undefined

7. In mathematics, a _____ number is a number which can be expressed as a ratio of two integers. Non-integer _____ numbers (commonly called fractions) are usually written as the vulgar fraction a / b, where b is not zero.
   a. Thing
   b. Rational0
   c. Undefined
   d. Undefined

8. A _____ decimal is a number whose decimal representation eventually becomes periodic (i.e. the same number sequence _____ indefinitely).
   a. Thing
   b. Repeating0
   c. Undefined
   d. Undefined

9. Mathematical _____ are the wide variety of ways to capture an abstract mathematical concept or relationship.
   a. Thing
   b. Representations0
   c. Undefined
   d. Undefined

10. A _____ decimal is a decimal fraction which ends after a definite number of digits.
    a. Thing
    b. Terminating0
    c. Undefined
    d. Undefined

11. A _____ is a quantity that denotes the proportional amount or magnitude of one quantity relative to another.

Chapter 1. A Precalculus Review

   a. Thing
   c. Undefined
   b. Ratio0
   d. Undefined

12. The _____ are the only integral domain whose positive elements are well-ordered, and in which order is preserved by addition. Like the natural numbers, the _____ form a countably infinite set. The set of all _____ is usually denoted in mathematics by a boldface Z .
   a. Integers0
   c. Undefined
   b. Thing
   d. Undefined

13. Recurring or _____ are numbers which when expressed as decimals have a set of "final" digits which repeat an infinite number of times.
   a. Thing
   c. Undefined
   b. Repeating decimals0
   d. Undefined

14. In mathematics, an _____ number is any real number that is not a rational number- that is, it is a number which cannot be expressed as a fraction m/n, where m and n are integers.
   a. Irrational0
   c. Undefined
   b. Thing
   d. Undefined

15. In mathematics, an _____ is any real number that is not a rational number ¡ª that is, it is a number which cannot be expressed as m/n, where m and n are integers.
   a. Thing
   c. Undefined
   b. Irrational number0
   d. Undefined

16. _____ are objects, characters, or other concrete representations of ideas, concepts, or other abstractions.
   a. Thing
   c. Undefined
   b. Symbols0
   d. Undefined

17. In mathematics, _____ are any real number that is not a rational number ¡ª that is, it is a number which cannot be expressed as m/n, where m and n are integers.
   a. Irrational numbers0
   c. Undefined
   b. Thing
   d. Undefined

18. The _____ (symbol _____) and the millibar (symbol mbar, also mb) are units of pressure.
   a. Thing
   c. Undefined
   b. Bar0
   d. Undefined

19. In geometry, an _____ is a point at which a line segment or ray terminates.
   a. Endpoint0
   c. Undefined
   b. Thing
   d. Undefined

20. In elementary algebra, an _____ is a set that contains every real number between two indicated numbers and may contain the two numbers themselves.
   a. Thing
   c. Undefined
   b. Interval0
   d. Undefined

21. In plane geometry, a _____ is a polygon with four equal sides, four right angles, and parallel opposite sides. In algebra, the _____ of a number is that number multiplied by itself.
   a. Square0
   b. Thing
   c. Undefined
   d. Undefined

22. _____ is the state of being greater than any finite number, however large.
   a. Infinity0
   b. Thing
   c. Undefined
   d. Undefined

23. A _____ is a symbolic representation denoting a quantity or expression. It often represents an "unknown" quantity that has the potential to change.
   a. Thing
   b. Variable0
   c. Undefined
   d. Undefined

24. _____ is a mathematical subject that includes the study of limits, derivatives, integrals, and power series and constitutes a major part of modern university curriculum.
   a. Thing
   b. Calculus0
   c. Undefined
   d. Undefined

25. Two mathematical objects are equal if and only if they are precisely the same in every way. This defines a binary relation, _____, denoted by the sign of _____ "=" in such a way that the statement "x = y" means that x and y are equal.
   a. Equality0
   b. Thing
   c. Undefined
   d. Undefined

26. A _____ is a set of possible values that a variable can take on in order to satisfy a given set of conditions, which may include equations and inequalities.
   a. Solution set0
   b. Thing
   c. Undefined
   d. Undefined

27. A _____ is a negotiable instrument instructing a financial institution to pay a specific amount of a specific currency from a specific demand account held in the maker/depositor's name with that institution. Both the maker and payee may be natural persons or legal entities.
   a. Thing
   b. Check0
   c. Undefined
   d. Undefined

28. _____ is a branch of mathematics concerning the study of structure, relation and quantity.
   a. Algebra0
   b. Concept
   c. Undefined
   d. Undefined

29. A _____ is a number that is less than zero.
   a. Negative number0
   b. Thing
   c. Undefined
   d. Undefined

30. In mathematics and the mathematical sciences, a _____ is a fixed, but possibly unspecified, value. This is in contrast to a variable, which is not fixed.

a. Constant0 b. Thing
c. Undefined d. Undefined

31. In mathematics, a _____ is an expression that is constructed from one or more variables and constants, using only the operations of addition, subtraction, multiplication, and constant positive whole number exponents. is a _____. Note in particular that division by an expression containing a variable is not in general allowed in polynomials. [1]
   a. Polynomial0 b. Thing
   c. Undefined d. Undefined

32. In mathematics, there are several meanings of _____ depending on the subject.
   a. Degree0 b. Thing
   c. Undefined d. Undefined

33. _____ means in succession or back-to-back
   a. Consecutive0 b. Thing
   c. Undefined d. Undefined

34. _____ is the application of tools and a processing medium to the transformation of raw materials into finished goods for sale.
   a. Thing b. Manufacturing0
   c. Undefined d. Undefined

35. The _____ of measurement are a globally standardized and modernized form of the metric system.
   a. Units0 b. Thing
   c. Undefined d. Undefined

36. A _____ is a function that assigns a number to subsets of a given set.
   a. Thing b. Measure0
   c. Undefined d. Undefined

37. In Euclidean geometry, a uniform _____ is a linear transformation that enlargers or diminishes objects, and whose _____ factor is the same in all directions. This is also called homothethy.
   a. Scale0 b. Thing
   c. Undefined d. Undefined

38. In mathematics, a _____ is the result of multiplying, or an expression that identifies factors to be multiplied.
   a. Thing b. Product0
   c. Undefined d. Undefined

39. _____, from Latin meaning "to make progress", is defined in two different ways. Pure economic _____ is the increase in wealth that an investor has from making an investment, taking into consideration all costs associated with that investment including the opportunity cost of capital.
   a. Profit0 b. Thing
   c. Undefined d. Undefined

40. In mathematics, an inequality is a statement about the relative size or order of two objects. For example 14 > 10, or 14 is _____ 10.
   a. Greater than0
   b. Thing
   c. Undefined
   d. Undefined

41. _____ is a business term for the amount of money that a company receives from its activities in a given period, mostly from sales of products and/or services to customers
   a. Thing
   b. Revenue0
   c. Undefined
   d. Undefined

42. A _____ is a special kind of ratio, indicating a relationship between two measurements with different units, such as miles to gallons or cents to pounds.
   a. Thing
   b. Rate0
   c. Undefined
   d. Undefined

43. _____ is the level of functional and/or metabolic efficiency of an organism at both the micro level.
   a. Health0
   b. Thing
   c. Undefined
   d. Undefined

44. In mathematics, the _____ of a function is the set of all "output" values produced by that function. Given a function $f : A \to B$, the _____ of f, is defined to be the set $\{x \in B : x = f(a) \text{ for some } a \in A\}$.
   a. Range0
   b. Thing
   c. Undefined
   d. Undefined

45. The metre (or _____, see spelling differences) is a measure of length. It is the basic unit of length in the metric system and in the International System of Units (SI), used around the world for general and scientific purposes.
   a. Concept
   b. Meter0
   c. Undefined
   d. Undefined

46. In common philosophical language, a proposition or _____, is the content of an assertion, that is, it is true-or-false and defined by the meaning of a particular piece of language.
   a. Statement0
   b. Concept
   c. Undefined
   d. Undefined

47. In mathematics, the _____ (or modulus) of a real number is its numerical value without regard to its sign.
   a. Thing
   b. Absolute value0
   c. Undefined
   d. Undefined

48. _____ is the middle point of a line segment.
   a. Midpoint0
   b. Thing
   c. Undefined
   d. Undefined

49. An _____ is a combination of numbers, operators, grouping symbols and/or free variables and bound variables arranged in a meaningful way which can be evaluated..

a. Thing
c. Undefined
b. Expression0
d. Undefined

50. _____, either of the curved-bracket punctuation marks that together make a set of _____
    a. Parentheses0
    b. Thing
    c. Undefined
    d. Undefined

51. In mathematics, a _____ of a number x is a number r such that r^2 = x, or in words, a number r whose square (the result of multiplying the number by itself) is x.
    a. Square root0
    b. Thing
    c. Undefined
    d. Undefined

52. In mathematics, a _____ of a complex-valued function f is a member x of the domain of f such that f(x) vanishes at x, that is, x : f (x) = 0.
    a. Thing
    b. Root0
    c. Undefined
    d. Undefined

53. In set theory and other branches of mathematics, the _____ of a collection of sets is the set that contains everything that belongs to any of the sets, but nothing else.
    a. Union0
    b. Thing
    c. Undefined
    d. Undefined

54. _____ is a way of expressing a number as a fraction of 100 per cent meaning "per hundred".
    a. Percent0
    b. Thing
    c. Undefined
    d. Undefined

55. A _____ is a statement or claimt that a particular event will occur in the future in more certain terms than a forecast.
    a. Prediction0
    b. Thing
    c. Undefined
    d. Undefined

56. _____ is a mathematical science pertaining to the collection, analysis, interpretation or explanation, and presentation of data. It is applicable to a wide variety of academic disciplines, from the physical and social sciences to the humanities.
    a. Statistics0
    b. Thing
    c. Undefined
    d. Undefined

57. In sociology and biology a _____ is the collection of people or organisms of a particular species living in a given geographic area or space, usually measured by a census.
    a. Population0
    b. Thing
    c. Undefined
    d. Undefined

58. _____ are any documents that aim to streamline particular processes according to a set routine.
    a. Guidelines0
    b. Thing
    c. Undefined
    d. Undefined

59. In geographic information systems, a _____ comprises an entity with a geographic location, typically determined by points, arcs, or polygons. Carriageways and cadastres exemplify _____ data.
   a. Thing
   b. Feature0
   c. Undefined
   d. Undefined

60. _____ of a random variable or somewhat more precisely, of a probability distribution is a measure of its statistical dispersion, indicating how its possible values are spread around the expected value.
   a. Thing
   b. Variance0
   c. Undefined
   d. Undefined

61. Mathematical _____ is used to represent ideas.
   a. Notation0
   b. Thing
   c. Undefined
   d. Undefined

62. _____ is a kind of property which exists as magnitude or multitude. It is among the basic classes of things along with quality, substance, change, and relation.
   a. Thing
   b. Amount0
   c. Undefined
   d. Undefined

63. In mathematics, a _____ is a condition that a solution to an optimization problem must satisfy in order to be acceptable.
   a. Thing
   b. Constraint0
   c. Undefined
   d. Undefined

64. _____ is the symbold used to indicate the nth root of a number
   a. Thing
   b. Radical0
   c. Undefined
   d. Undefined

65. In mathematics, _____ are used to indicate the square root of a number.
   a. Radicals0
   b. Thing
   c. Undefined
   d. Undefined

66. _____ is a mathematical operation, written a^n, involving two numbers, the base a and the exponent n.
   a. Thing
   b. Exponentiating0
   c. Undefined
   d. Undefined

67. _____ is a mathematical operation, written a^n, involving two numbers, the base a and the exponent n.
   a. Exponentiation0
   b. Thing
   c. Undefined
   d. Undefined

68. An _____ of a number *a* is a number *b* such that $b^n=a$.
   a. Thing
   b. Nth root0
   c. Undefined
   d. Undefined

Chapter 1. A Precalculus Review

69. In mathematics, factorization (British English: factorisation) or factoring is the decomposition of an object (for example, a number, a polynomial, or a matrix) into a product of other objects, or _____, which when multiplied together give the original.
    a. Thing
    b. Factors0
    c. Undefined
    d. Undefined

70. The _____ of a ring R is defined to be the smallest positive integer n such that $n\, a = 0$, for all a in R.
    a. Thing
    b. Characteristic0
    c. Undefined
    d. Undefined

71. A _____ is the result of the addition of a set of numbers. The numbers may be natural numbers, complex numbers, matrices, or still more complicated objects. An infinite _____ is a subtle procedure known as a series.
    a. Thing
    b. Sum0
    c. Undefined
    d. Undefined

72. In mathematics, and in particular in abstract algebra, the _____ is a property of binary operations that generalises the distributive law from elementary algebra.
    a. Distributive property0
    b. Thing
    c. Undefined
    d. Undefined

73. In mathematics, _____ is the decomposition of an object into a product of other objects, or factors, which when multiplied together give the original.
    a. Thing
    b. Factoring0
    c. Undefined
    d. Undefined

74. The _____ is a measurement of how a function changes when the values of its inputs change.
    a. Derivative0
    b. Thing
    c. Undefined
    d. Undefined

75. Equivalence is the condition of being _____ or essentially equal.
    a. Equivalent0
    b. Thing
    c. Undefined
    d. Undefined

76. In mathematics, a _____ is the end result of a division problem. It can also be expressed as the number of times the divisor divides into the dividend.
    a. Thing
    b. Quotient0
    c. Undefined
    d. Undefined

77. An _____ of a function f is a function F whose derivative is equal to f, i.e., F' = f.
    a. Thing
    b. Antiderivative0
    c. Undefined
    d. Undefined

78. In physics, a _____ may refer to the scalar _____ or to the vector _____.
    a. Thing
    b. Potential0
    c. Undefined
    d. Undefined

Chapter 1. A Precalculus Review

79. In mathematics, a _____ of a k-place relation L ⊆ X_1 × ... × X_k is one of the sets X_j, 1 ≤ j ≤ k. In the special case where k = 2 and L ⊆ X_1 × X_2 is a function L : X_1 → X_2, it is conventional to refer to X_1 as the _____ of the function and to refer to X_2 as the codomain of the function.
- a. Domain0
- b. Thing
- c. Undefined
- d. Undefined

80. A _____ or CD is a time deposit, a financial product commonly offered to consumers by banks, thrift institutions, and credit unions.
- a. Certificate of deposit0
- b. Thing
- c. Undefined
- d. Undefined

81. _____ is an expression of the effective interest rate that will be paid on a loan, taking into account one-time fees and standardizing the way the rate is expressed.
- a. Thing
- b. Annual percentage rate0
- c. Undefined
- d. Undefined

82. _____ is the fee paid on borrowed money.
- a. Interest0
- b. Thing
- c. Undefined
- d. Undefined

83. _____ interest refers to the fact that whenever interest is calculated, it is based not only on the original principal, but also on any unpaid interest that has been added to the principal.
- a. Thing
- b. Compound0
- c. Undefined
- d. Undefined

84. _____ refers to the fact that whenever interest is calculated, it is based not only on the original principal, but also on any unpaid interest that has been added to the principal. The more frequently interest is compounded, the faster the balance grows.
- a. Compound interest0
- b. Concept
- c. Undefined
- d. Undefined

85. In banking and accountancy, the outstanding _____ is the amount of money owned, or due, that remains in a deposit account or a loan account at a given date, after all past remittances, payments and withdrawal have been accounted for.
- a. Balance0
- b. Thing
- c. Undefined
- d. Undefined

86. A _____ is an object that is attached to a pivot point so that it can swing freely.
- a. Pendulum0
- b. Thing
- c. Undefined
- d. Undefined

87. In business, particularly accounting, a _____ is the time intervals that the accounts, statement, payments, or other calculations cover.
- a. Period0
- b. Thing
- c. Undefined
- d. Undefined

Chapter 1. A Precalculus Review

88. _____ is the income from capital investment paid in a series of regular payments.
    a. Annuity0
    b. Thing
    c. Undefined
    d. Undefined

89. In mathematics, _____ allows the rapid division of any polynomial by a binomial of the form x − r. It was described by Paolo Ruffini in 1809. _____ is a special case of long division when the divisor is a linear factor.
    a. Thing
    b. Ruffini's rule0
    c. Undefined
    d. Undefined

90. In mathematics, a _____ is a statement that can be proved on the basis of explicitly stated or previously agreed assumptions.
    a. Theorem0
    b. Thing
    c. Undefined
    d. Undefined

91. In number theory, the _____ of arithmetic (or unique factorization theorem) states that every natural number greater than 1 can be written as a unique product of prime numbers.
    a. Fundamental theorem0
    b. Concept
    c. Undefined
    d. Undefined

92. _____ states that every non-zero single-variable polynomial, with complex coefficients, has exactly as many complex roots as its degree, if repeated roots are counted up to their multiplicity.
    a. Fundamental theorem of algebra0
    b. Thing
    c. Undefined
    d. Undefined

93. The word _____ comes from the Latin word linearis, which means created by lines.
    a. Thing
    b. Linear0
    c. Undefined
    d. Undefined

94. A quadratic equation with real solutions, called roots, which may be real or complex, is given by the _____: $x = \frac{-b \pm \sqrt{b^2 - 4ac}}{2a}$.
    a. Quadratic formula0
    b. Thing
    c. Undefined
    d. Undefined

95. In mathematics, a _____ is a polynomial equation of the second degree. The general form is $ax^2 + bx + c = 0$.
    a. Thing
    b. Quadratic equation0
    c. Undefined
    d. Undefined

96. In mathematics, an _____ number is a complex number whose square is a negative real number. They were defined in 1572 by Rafael Bombelli.
    a. Imaginary0
    b. Thing
    c. Undefined
    d. Undefined

97. In mathematics, a _____ is a constant multiplicative factor of a certain object. The object can be such things as a variable, a vector, a function, etc. For example, the _____ of $9x^2$ is 9.

a. Thing
b. Coefficient0
c. Undefined
d. Undefined

98. In arithmetic, _____ is a procedure for calculating the division of one integer, called the dividend, by another integer called the divisor, to produce a result called the quotient.
a. Thing
b. Long division0
c. Undefined
d. Undefined

99. The _____ is the maximum of the degrees of all terms in the polynomial.
a. Thing
b. Degree of a polynomial0
c. Undefined
d. Undefined

100. In mathematics, a _____ of an integer n, also called a factor of n, is an integer which evenly divides n without leaving a remainder.
a. Divisor0
b. Thing
c. Undefined
d. Undefined

101. _____ is a fixed, but possibly unspecified, value. This is in contrast to a variable, which is not fixed.
a. Constant term0
b. Thing
c. Undefined
d. Undefined

102. In mathematics, an _____, mean, or central tendency of a data set refers to a measure of the "middle" or "expected" value of the data set.
a. Concept
b. Average0
c. Undefined
d. Undefined

103. A _____ is a numeral used to indicate a count. The most common use of the word today is to name the part of a fraction that tells the number or count of equal parts.
a. Numerator0
b. Thing
c. Undefined
d. Undefined

104. A _____ is the part of a fraction that tells how many equal parts make up a whole, and which is used in the name of the fraction: "halves", "thirds", "fourths" or "quarters", "fifths" and so on.
a. Denominator0
b. Concept
c. Undefined
d. Undefined

105. A _____ fraction is a fraction in which the absolute value of the numerator is less than the denominator--hence, the absolute value of the fraction is less than 1.
a. Proper0
b. Thing
c. Undefined
d. Undefined

106. _____ is the largest positive integer that divides both numbers without remainder.
a. Thing
b. Common Factor0
c. Undefined
d. Undefined

107. _____ in mathematics is the process of removing a square root or imaginary number from the denominator of a fraction. See conjugate and complex conjugate.
   a. Rationalization0
   b. Thing
   c. Undefined
   d. Undefined

108. _____, a field in mathematics, is the study of how functions change when their inputs change. The primary object of study in _____ is the derivative.
   a. Differential calculus0
   b. Thing
   c. Undefined
   d. Undefined

109. _____, or Rationalisation in mathematics is the process of removing a square root or imaginary number from the denominator of a fraction.
   a. Thing
   b. Rationalizing0
   c. Undefined
   d. Undefined

110. A _____ is a type of debt. All material things can be lent but this article focuses exclusively on monetary loans. Like all debt instruments, a _____ entails the redistribution of financial assets over time, between the lender and the borrower.
   a. Loan0
   b. Thing
   c. Undefined
   d. Undefined

111. Order theory is a branch of mathematics that studies various kinds of binary relations that capture the intuitive notion of a mathematical _____.
   a. Thing
   b. Ordering0
   c. Undefined
   d. Undefined

112. _____ is a list of goods and materials, or those goods and materials themselves, held available in stock by a business
   a. Thing
   b. Inventory0
   c. Undefined
   d. Undefined

Chapter 2. Functions, Graphs, and Limits

1. A _____ is a set of numbers that designate location in a given reference system, such as x,y in a planar _____ system or an x,y,z in a three-dimensional _____ system.
   a. Coordinate0
   b. Thing
   c. Undefined
   d. Undefined

2. In mathematics, a _____ is a two-dimensional manifold or surface that is perfectly flat.
   a. Plane0
   b. Thing
   c. Undefined
   d. Undefined

3. In geometry, a line _____ is a part of a line that is bounded by two end points, and contains every point on the line between its end points.
   a. Concept
   b. Segment0
   c. Undefined
   d. Undefined

4. A _____ is a part of a line that is bounded by two end points, and contains every point on the line between its end points.
   a. Thing
   b. Line segment0
   c. Undefined
   d. Undefined

5. _____ is the middle point of a line segment.
   a. Midpoint0
   b. Thing
   c. Undefined
   d. Undefined

6. A _____ consists of one quarter of the coordinate plane.
   a. Thing
   b. Quadrant0
   c. Undefined
   d. Undefined

7. In mathematics and its applications, a _____ is a system for assigning an n-tuple of numbers or scalars to each point in an n-dimensional space.
   a. Concept
   b. Coordinate system0
   c. Undefined
   d. Undefined

8. A _____ is a one-dimensional picture in which the integers are shown as specially-marked points evenly spaced on a line.
   a. Number line0
   b. Thing
   c. Undefined
   d. Undefined

9. In mathematics, a _____ may be described informally as a number that can be given by an infinite decimal representation.
   a. Real number0
   b. Thing
   c. Undefined
   d. Undefined

10. An _____ is a collection of two not necessarily distinct objects, one of which is distinguished as the first coordinate and the other as the second coordinate.
    a. Thing
    b. Ordered pair0
    c. Undefined
    d. Undefined

Chapter 2. Functions, Graphs, and Limits

11. In mathematics, the conjugate _____ or adjoint matrix of an m-by-n matrix A with complex entries is the n-by-m matrix A* obtained from A by taking the transpose and then taking the complex conjugate of each entry.
    a. Thing
    b. Pairs0
    c. Undefined
    d. Undefined

12. _____ means of or relating to the French philosopher and mathematician René Descartes.
    a. Cartesian0
    b. Thing
    c. Undefined
    d. Undefined

13. _____ was a highly influential French philosopher, mathematician, scientist, and writer. Dubbed the "Founder of Modern Philosophy", and the "Father of Modern Mathematics". His theories provided the basis for the calculus of Newton and Leibniz, by applying infinitesimal calculus to the tangent line problem, thus permitting the evolution of that branch of modern mathematics
    a. Person
    b. Descartes0
    c. Undefined
    d. Undefined

14. An _____ is when two lines intersect somewhere on a plane creating a right angle at intersection
    a. Axes0
    b. Thing
    c. Undefined
    d. Undefined

15. In mathematics, the _____ of a coordinate system is the point where the axes of the system intersect.
    a. Origin0
    b. Thing
    c. Undefined
    d. Undefined

16. In mathematics, the _____ of two sets A and B is the set that contains all elements of A that also belong to B (or equivalently, all elements of B that also belong to A), but no other elements.
    a. Intersection0
    b. Thing
    c. Undefined
    d. Undefined

17. In astronomy, geography, geometry and related sciences and contexts, a plane is said to be _____ at a given point if it is locally perpendicular to the gradient of the gravity field, i.e., with the direction of the gravitational force at that point.
    a. Thing
    b. Horizontal0
    c. Undefined
    d. Undefined

18. A _____ is a symbolic representation denoting a quantity or expression. It often represents an "unknown" quantity that has the potential to change.
    a. Variable0
    b. Thing
    c. Undefined
    d. Undefined

19. In geometry, the _____ of an object is a point in some sense in the middle of the object.
    a. Center0
    b. Thing
    c. Undefined
    d. Undefined

20. _____ is a mathematical science pertaining to the collection, analysis, interpretation or explanation, and presentation of data. It is applicable to a wide variety of academic disciplines, from the physical and social sciences to the humanities.

Chapter 2. Functions, Graphs, and Limits

a. Statistics0
b. Thing
c. Undefined
d. Undefined

21. _____ is a synonym for information.
   a. Thing
   b. Data0
   c. Undefined
   d. Undefined

22. An _____ is a straight line around which a geometric figure can be rotated.
   a. Thing
   b. Axis0
   c. Undefined
   d. Undefined

23. _____ is a kind of property which exists as magnitude or multitude. It is among the basic classes of things along with quality, substance, change, and relation.
   a. Amount0
   b. Thing
   c. Undefined
   d. Undefined

24. A _____, scatter diagram or scatter graph is a chart that uses Cartesian coordinates to display values for two variables.
   a. Thing
   b. Scatter plot0
   c. Undefined
   d. Undefined

25. Mathematical _____ are the wide variety of ways to capture an abstract mathematical concept or relationship.
   a. Representations0
   b. Thing
   c. Undefined
   d. Undefined

26. A _____ is one of the basic shapes of geometry: a polygon with three vertices and three sides which are straight line segments.
   a. Triangle0
   b. Thing
   c. Undefined
   d. Undefined

27. _____ is a relation in Euclidean geometry among the three sides of a right triangle.
   a. Thing
   b. Pythagorean Theorem0
   c. Undefined
   d. Undefined

28. In geometry, a _____ is a special kind of point, usually a corner of a polygon, polyhedron, or higher dimensional polytope. In the geometry of curves a _____ is a point of where the first derivative of curvature is zero. In graph theory, a _____ is the fundamental unit out of which graphs are formed
   a. Vertex0
   b. Thing
   c. Undefined
   d. Undefined

29. _____ has one 90° internal angle a right angle.
   a. Right triangle0
   b. Thing
   c. Undefined
   d. Undefined

30. In mathematics, a _____ is a statement that can be proved on the basis of explicitly stated or previously agreed assumptions.

a. Thing
b. Theorem0
c. Undefined
d. Undefined

31. In Euclidean geometry, a uniform _____ is a linear transformation that enlargers or diminishes objects, and whose _____ factor is the same in all directions. This is also called homothethy.
   a. Thing
   b. Scale0
   c. Undefined
   d. Undefined

32. In geometry, an _____ is a point at which a line segment or ray terminates.
   a. Endpoint0
   b. Thing
   c. Undefined
   d. Undefined

33. _____ are the basic objects of study in graph theory. Informally speaking, a graph is a set of objects called points, nodes, or vertices connected by links called lines or edges.
   a. Graphs0
   b. Thing
   c. Undefined
   d. Undefined

34. In mathematics, an _____, mean, or central tendency of a data set refers to a measure of the "middle" or "expected" value of the data set.
   a. Concept
   b. Average0
   c. Undefined
   d. Undefined

35. The mathematical concept of a _____ expresses the intuitive idea of deterministic dependence between two quantities, one of which is viewed as primary and the other as secondary. A _____ then is a way to associate a unique output for each input of a specified type, for example, a real number or an element of a given set.
   a. Function0
   b. Thing
   c. Undefined
   d. Undefined

36. The word _____ comes from the Latin word linearis, which means created by lines.
   a. Thing
   b. Linear0
   c. Undefined
   d. Undefined

37. A _____ is a four-sided plane figure that has two sets of opposite parallel sides.
   a. Parallelogram0
   b. Concept
   c. Undefined
   d. Undefined

38. A _____ (or shape) refers to the external two-dimensional outline, appearance or configuration of some thing - in contrast to the matter or content or substance of which it is composed.
   a. Plane figure0
   b. Thing
   c. Undefined
   d. Undefined

39. The _____ of measurement are a globally standardized and modernized form of the metric system.
   a. Units0
   b. Thing
   c. Undefined
   d. Undefined

Chapter 2. Functions, Graphs, and Limits

40. In mathematics, a _____ in elementary terms is any of a variety of different functions from geometry, such as rotations, reflections and translations.
    a. Thing
    b. Transformation0
    c. Undefined
    d. Undefined

41. _____ is a set, with some particular properties and usually some additional structure, such as the operations of addition or multiplication, for instance.
    a. Space0
    b. Thing
    c. Undefined
    d. Undefined

42. In geometry, two sets are called _____ if one can be transformed into the other by an isometry, i.e., a combination of translations, rotations and reflections.
    a. Thing
    b. Congruent0
    c. Undefined
    d. Undefined

43. The _____ (symbol _____) and the millibar (symbol mbar, also mb) are units of pressure.
    a. Thing
    b. Bar0
    c. Undefined
    d. Undefined

44. A bar chart, also known as a _____, is a chart with rectangular bars of lengths usually proportional to the magnitudes or frequencies of what they represent.
    a. Thing
    b. Bar graph0
    c. Undefined
    d. Undefined

45. In architecture and structural engineering, a _____ is a structure comprising one or more triangular units which are constructed with straight slender members whose ends are connected at joints.
    a. Thing
    b. Truss0
    c. Undefined
    d. Undefined

46. In plane geometry, a _____ is a polygon with four equal sides, four right angles, and parallel opposite sides. In algebra, the _____ of a number is that number multiplied by itself.
    a. Square0
    b. Thing
    c. Undefined
    d. Undefined

47. _____ is a branch of mathematics concerning the study of structure, relation and quantity.
    a. Concept
    b. Algebra0
    c. Undefined
    d. Undefined

48. _____, also referred to as common or ordinary shares, are, as the name implies, the most usual and commonly held form of stock in a corporation
    a. Common stock0
    b. Thing
    c. Undefined
    d. Undefined

49. _____ is a way of expressing a number as a fraction of 100 per cent meaning "per hundred".

Chapter 2. Functions, Graphs, and Limits

a. Percent0
b. Thing
c. Undefined
d. Undefined

50. Compass and straightedge or ruler-and-compass _____ is the _____ of lengths or angles using only an idealized ruler and compass.
   a. Thing
   b. Construction0
   c. Undefined
   d. Undefined

51. _____, from Latin meaning "to make progress", is defined in two different ways. Pure economic _____ is the increase in wealth that an investor has from making an investment, taking into consideration all costs associated with that investment including the opportunity cost of capital.
   a. Profit0
   b. Thing
   c. Undefined
   d. Undefined

52. _____ is a business term for the amount of money that a company receives from its activities in a given period, mostly from sales of products and/or services to customers
   a. Thing
   b. Revenue0
   c. Undefined
   d. Undefined

53. In mathematics, the concept of a _____ tries to capture the intuitive idea of a geometrical one-dimensional and continuous object. A simple example is the circle.
   a. Curve0
   b. Thing
   c. Undefined
   d. Undefined

54. In mathematics, _____ are the intuitive idea of a geometrical one-dimensional and continuous object.
   a. Curves0
   b. Thing
   c. Undefined
   d. Undefined

55. Any point where a graph makes contact with an coordinate axis is called an _____ of the graph
   a. Thing
   b. Intercept0
   c. Undefined
   d. Undefined

56. In linear algebra, the _____ of an n-by-n square matrix A is defined to be the sum of the elements on the main diagonal of A,
   a. Trace0
   b. Thing
   c. Undefined
   d. Undefined

57. In geographic information systems, a _____ comprises an entity with a geographic location, typically determined by points, arcs, or polygons. Carriageways and cadastres exemplify _____ data.
   a. Thing
   b. Feature0
   c. Undefined
   d. Undefined

58. In Euclidean geometry, a _____ is the set of all points in a plane at a fixed distance, called the radius, from a given point, the center.

Chapter 2. Functions, Graphs, and Limits

    a. Circle0
    b. Thing
    c. Undefined
    d. Undefined

59. _____ is a notation for writing numbers that is often used by scientists and mathematicians to make it easier to write large and small numbers.
    a. Scientific notation0
    b. Thing
    c. Undefined
    d. Undefined

60. In classical geometry, a _____ of a circle or sphere is any line segment from its center to its boundary. By extension, the _____ of a circle or sphere is the length of any such segment. The _____ is half the diameter. In science and engineering the term _____ of curvature is commonly used as a synonym for _____.
    a. Radius0
    b. Thing
    c. Undefined
    d. Undefined

61. In mathematics, a _____ is the result of multiplying, or an expression that identifies factors to be multiplied.
    a. Product0
    b. Thing
    c. Undefined
    d. Undefined

62. Initial objects are also called _____, and terminal objects are also called final.
    a. Thing
    b. Coterminal0
    c. Undefined
    d. Undefined

63. _____ or investing is a term with several closely-related meanings in business management, finance and economics, related to saving or deferring consumption.
    a. Investment0
    b. Thing
    c. Undefined
    d. Undefined

64. In economics, economic _____ is simply a state of the world where economic forces are balanced and in the absence of external influences the values of economic variables will not change.
    a. Thing
    b. Equilibrium0
    c. Undefined
    d. Undefined

65. In economics, supply and _____ describe market relations between prospective sellers and buyers of a good.
    a. Demand0
    b. Thing
    c. Undefined
    d. Undefined

66. _____ can be defined as the graph depicting the relationship between the price of a certain commodity, and the amount of it that consumers are willing and able to purchase at that given price demand.
    a. Demand curve0
    b. Thing
    c. Undefined
    d. Undefined

67. In economics, _____ describe market relations between prospective sellers and buyers of a good.
    a. Thing
    b. Supply and demand0
    c. Undefined
    d. Undefined

68. In mathematics, factorization (British English: factorisation) or factoring is the decomposition of an object (for example, a number, a polynomial, or a matrix) into a product of other objects, or _____, which when multiplied together give the original.
   a. Thing
   b. Factors0
   c. Undefined
   d. Undefined

69. _____ is the price at which the quantity demanded of a good or service is equal to the quantity supplied.
   a. Equilibrium price0
   b. Thing
   c. Undefined
   d. Undefined

70. A _____ is an abstract model that uses mathematical language to describe the behavior of a system. Eykhoff defined a _____ as 'a representation of the essential aspects of an existing system which presents knowledge of that system in usable form'.
   a. Thing
   b. Mathematical model0
   c. Undefined
   d. Undefined

71. In mathematics, a _____ is any one of several different types of functions, mappings, operations, or transformations.
   a. Thing
   b. Projection0
   c. Undefined
   d. Undefined

72. In regression analysis, _____, also known as ordinary _____ analysis is a method for linear regression that determines the values of unknown quantities in a statistical model by minimizing the sum of the residuals difference between the predicted and observed values squared.
   a. Thing
   b. Least squares0
   c. Undefined
   d. Undefined

73. _____ is a mathematical subject that includes the study of limits, derivatives, integrals, and power series and constitutes a major part of modern university curriculum.
   a. Thing
   b. Calculus0
   c. Undefined
   d. Undefined

74. One of the three formats applicable to a quadratic function is the _____ which is defined as $f = ax^2 + bx + c$.
   a. Thing
   b. General form0
   c. Undefined
   d. Undefined

75. In geometry, a _____ (Greek words diairo = divide and metro = measure) of a circle is any straight line segment that passes through the centre and whose endpoints are on the circular boundary, or, in more modern usage, the length of such a line segment. When using the word in the more modern sense, one speaks of the _____ rather than a _____, because all diameters of a circle have the same length. This length is twice the radius. The _____ of a circle is also the longest chord that the circle has.
   a. Thing
   b. Diameter0
   c. Undefined
   d. Undefined

Chapter 2. Functions, Graphs, and Limits 21

76. A _____ is a unit of length, usually used to measure distance, in a number of different systems, including Imperial units, United States customary units and Norwegian/Swedish mil. Its size can vary from system to system, but in each is between 1 and 10 kilometers. In contemporary English contexts _____ refers to either:
   a. Thing
   b. Mile0
   c. Undefined
   d. Undefined

77. U.S. liquid _____ is legally defined as 231 cubic inches, and is equal to 3.785411784 litres or abotu 0.13368 cubic feet. This is the most common definition of a _____. The U.S. fluid ounce is defined as 1/128 of a U.S. _____.
   a. Gallon0
   b. Thing
   c. Undefined
   d. Undefined

78. In mathematics, a _____ is a mathematical statement which appears likely to be true, but has not been formally proven to be true under the rules of mathematical logic.
   a. Concept
   b. Conjecture0
   c. Undefined
   d. Undefined

79. A frame of _____ is a particular perspective from which the universe is observed.
   a. Reference0
   b. Thing
   c. Undefined
   d. Undefined

80. _____ is often used to describe the measurement of the steepness, incline, gradient, or grade of a straight line. The _____ is defined as the ratio of the "rise" divided by the "run" between two points on a line, or in other words, the ratio of the altitude change to the horizontal distance between any two points on the line.
   a. Slope0
   b. Thing
   c. Undefined
   d. Undefined

81. A _____ is an equation in which each term is either a constant or the product of a constant times the first power of a variable.
   a. Thing
   b. Linear equation0
   c. Undefined
   d. Undefined

82. In geometry, two lines or planes if one falls on the other in such a way as to create congruent adjacent angles. The term may be used as a noun or adjective. Thus, referring to Figure 1, the line AB is the _____ to CD through the point B.
   a. Perpendicular0
   b. Thing
   c. Undefined
   d. Undefined

83. In mathematics, defined and _____ are used to explain whether or not expressions have meaningful, sensible, and unambiguous values.
   a. Undefined0
   b. Thing
   c. Undefined
   d. Undefined

84. A _____ is a special kind of ratio, indicating a relationship between two measurements with different units, such as miles to gallons or cents to pounds.

a. Rate0
b. Thing
c. Undefined
d. Undefined

85. A _____ is a quantity that denotes the proportional amount or magnitude of one quantity relative to another.
    a. Thing
    b. Ratio0
    c. Undefined
    d. Undefined

86. A _____ is a function that assigns a number to subsets of a given set.
    a. Thing
    b. Measure0
    c. Undefined
    d. Undefined

87. Fixed costs are expenses whose total does not change in proportion to the activity of a business.Unit fixed costs decline with volume following a retangular hyperbola as the volume of production.Variable costs by contrast change in relation to the activity of a business such as sales or production volume.Along with variable costs,fixed costs make up one of the two components of total cost. In the most simple production function total cost is equal to fixed costs plus variable costs.In accounting terminology, fixed costs will broadly include all costs which are not included in cost of goods sold, and variable costs are those captured in costs of goods sold. The implicit assumption required to make the equivalence between the accounting and economics terminology is that the accounting period is equal to the period in which fixed costs do not vary in relation to production. In practice, this equivalence does not always hold and depending on the period under consideration by management, some overhead expenses can be adjusted by management, and the specific allocation of each expense to each category will be decided under cost accounting.In business planning and management accounting, usage of the terms fixed costs, variable costs and others will often differ from usage in economics, and may depend on the intended use. For example, costs may be segregated into per unit costs fixed costs per period, and variable costs as a proportion of revenue. Capital expenditures will usually be allocated separately, and depending on the purpose, a portion may be regularly allocated to expenses as depreciation and amortization and seen as a _____ per period, or the entire amount may be considered upfront fixed costs.
    a. Thing
    b. Fixed cost0
    c. Undefined
    d. Undefined

88. In finance, a _____ is collateral that the holder of a position in securities, options, or futures contracts has to deposit to cover the credit risk of his counterparty.
    a. Thing
    b. Margin0
    c. Undefined
    d. Undefined

89. A _____ is a numeral used to indicate a count. The most common use of the word today is to name the part of a fraction that tells the number or count of equal parts.
    a. Thing
    b. Numerator0
    c. Undefined
    d. Undefined

90. A _____ is the part of a fraction that tells how many equal parts make up a whole, and which is used in the name of the fraction: "halves", "thirds", "fourths" or "quarters", "fifths" and so on.
    a. Concept
    b. Denominator0
    c. Undefined
    d. Undefined

91. _____ is the calculated approximation of a result which is usable even if input data may be incomplete, uncertain, or noisy.

Chapter 2. Functions, Graphs, and Limits

a. Estimation0
b. Concept
c. Undefined
d. Undefined

92. In mathematics, _____ is the process of constructing new data points outside a discrete set of known data points. It is similar to the process of interpolation, which constructs new points between known points, but its results are often less meaningful, and are subject to greater uncertainty.
   a. Thing
   b. Extrapolation0
   c. Undefined
   d. Undefined

93. _____ the expected value of a random variable displays the average or central value of the variable. It is a summary value of the distribution of the variable.
   a. Thing
   b. Determining0
   c. Undefined
   d. Undefined

94. _____ is a method of constructing new data points from a discrete set of known data points.
   a. Thing
   b. Interpolation0
   c. Undefined
   d. Undefined

95. _____ is a term used in accounting, economics and finance with reference to the fact that assets with finite lives lose value over time.
   a. Thing
   b. Depreciation0
   c. Undefined
   d. Undefined

96. The _____ is the United States federal government agency that collects taxes and enforces the internal revenue laws.
   a. Thing
   b. Internal Revenue Service0
   c. Undefined
   d. Undefined

97. An _____ is a combination of numbers, operators, grouping symbols and/or free variables and bound variables arranged in a meaningful way which can be evaluated..
   a. Expression0
   b. Thing
   c. Undefined
   d. Undefined

98. In sociology and biology a _____ is the collection of people or organisms of a particular species living in a given geographic area or space, usually measured by a census.
   a. Population0
   b. Thing
   c. Undefined
   d. Undefined

99. _____ is a form of periodic payment from an employer to an employee, which is specified in an employment contract.
   a. Thing
   b. Gross pay0
   c. Undefined
   d. Undefined

100. A _____ is a form of periodic payment from an employer to an employee, which is specified in an employment contract.

Chapter 2. Functions, Graphs, and Limits

    a. Salary0   b. Thing
    c. Undefined   d. Undefined

101. In set theory and other branches of mathematics, the _____ of a collection of sets is the set that contains everything that belongs to any of the sets, but nothing else.
    a. Union0   b. Thing
    c. Undefined   d. Undefined

102. A _____ is a compensation which workers receive in exchange for their labor.
    a. Wage0   b. Thing
    c. Undefined   d. Undefined

103. In mathematics, in the field of group theory, a _____ of a group is a quasisimple subnormal subgroup.
    a. Concept   b. Component0
    c. Undefined   d. Undefined

104. _____ is a physical property of a system that underlies the common notions of hot and cold; something that is hotter has the greater _____.
    a. Thing   b. Temperature0
    c. Undefined   d. Undefined

105. The metre (or _____, see spelling differences) is a measure of length. It is the basic unit of length in the metric system and in the International System of Units (SI), used around the world for general and scientific purposes.
    a. Meter0   b. Concept
    c. Undefined   d. Undefined

106. A _____ is an individual or household that purchases and uses goods and services generated within the economy.
    a. Consumer0   b. Thing
    c. Undefined   d. Undefined

107. _____ consists of the knowledge of various products to protect the public from fraudulent or unforseeable circumstances.
    a. Consumer awareness0   b. Thing
    c. Undefined   d. Undefined

108. The payment of _____ as remuneration for services rendered or products sold is a common way to reward sales people.
    a. Commission0   b. Thing
    c. Undefined   d. Undefined

109. In mathematics, an _____ is any of the arguments, i.e. "inputs", to a function. Thus if we have a function f(x), then x is a _____.
    a. Thing   b. Independent variable0
    c. Undefined   d. Undefined

Chapter 2. Functions, Graphs, and Limits

110. In a function the _____, is the variable which is the value, i.e. the "output", of the function.
   a. Dependent variable0
   b. Thing
   c. Undefined
   d. Undefined

111. In mathematics, a _____ of a k-place relation $L \subseteq X_1 \times \ldots \times X_k$ is one of the sets X_j, $1 \leq j \leq k$. In the special case where k = 2 and $L \subseteq X_1 \times X_2$ is a function $L : X_1 \to X_2$, it is conventional to refer to X_1 as the _____ of the function and to refer to X_2 as the codomain of the function.
   a. Thing
   b. Domain0
   c. Undefined
   d. Undefined

112. In mathematics, the _____ of a function is the set of all "output" values produced by that function. Given a function $f : A \to B$, the _____ of f, is defined to be the set $\{x \in B : x = f(a)$ for some $a \in A\}$.
   a. Thing
   b. Range0
   c. Undefined
   d. Undefined

113. The _____, the average in everyday English, which is also called the arithmetic _____ (and is distinguished from the geometric _____ or harmonic _____). The average is also called the sample _____. The expected value of a random variable, which is also called the population _____.
   a. Mean0
   b. Thing
   c. Undefined
   d. Undefined

114. A _____ is a simplified and structured visual representation of concepts, ideas, constructions, relations, statistical data, anatomy etc used in all aspects of human activities to visualize and clarify the topic.
   a. Thing
   b. Diagram0
   c. Undefined
   d. Undefined

115. In mathematics, the _____ f is the collection of all ordered pairs . In particular, graph means the graphical representation of this collection, in the form of a curve or surface, together with axes, etc. Graphing on a Cartesian plane is sometimes referred to as curve sketching.
   a. Graph of a function0
   b. Thing
   c. Undefined
   d. Undefined

116. In financial mathematics, the _____ volatility of an option contract is the volatility _____ by the market price of the option based on an option pricing model.
   a. Implied0
   b. Thing
   c. Undefined
   d. Undcfincd

117. A _____ is a number that is less than zero.
   a. Thing
   b. Negative number0
   c. Undefined
   d. Undefined

118. In mathematics, a _____ of a complex-valued function f is a member x of the domain of f such that f(x) vanishes at x, that is, $x : f(x) = 0$.
   a. Thing
   b. Root0
   c. Undefined
   d. Undefined

Chapter 2. Functions, Graphs, and Limits

119. In elementary algebra, an _____ is a set that contains every real number between two indicated numbers and may contain the two numbers themselves.
   a. Interval0
   b. Thing
   c. Undefined
   d. Undefined

120. Mathematical _____ is used to represent ideas.
   a. Notation0
   b. Thing
   c. Undefined
   d. Undefined

121. _____ is a test used to determine if a function is injective, surjective or bijective.
   a. Horizontal line test0
   b. Thing
   c. Undefined
   d. Undefined

122. Acid _____ ratio measures the ability of a company to use its near cash or quick assets to immediately extinguish its current liabilities.
   a. Thing
   b. Test0
   c. Undefined
   d. Undefined

123. _____, either of the curved-bracket punctuation marks that together make a set of _____
   a. Thing
   b. Parentheses0
   c. Undefined
   d. Undefined

124. In mathematics, a _____ is the end result of a division problem. It can also be expressed as the number of times the divisor divides into the dividend.
   a. Quotient0
   b. Thing
   c. Undefined
   d. Undefined

125. The function difference divided by the point difference is known as the _____
   a. Thing
   b. Difference quotient0
   c. Undefined
   d. Undefined

126. A _____ number is a positive integer which has a positive divisor other than one or itself.
   a. Thing
   b. Composite0
   c. Undefined
   d. Undefined

127. A _____, formed by the composition of one function on another, represents the application of the former to the result of the application of the latter to the argument of the composite.
   a. Composite function0
   b. Thing
   c. Undefined
   d. Undefined

128. _____ element of an element x with respect to a binary operation * with identity element e is an element y such that x * y = y * x = e. In particular,
   a. Inverse0
   b. Thing
   c. Undefined
   d. Undefined

129. An _____ is a function which does the reverse of a given function.

a. Inverse function0
b. Thing
c. Undefined
d. Undefined

130. A _____ is a negotiable instrument instructing a financial institution to pay a specific amount of a specific currency from a specific demand account held in the maker/depositor's name with that institution. Both the maker and payee may be natural persons or legal entities.
  a. Thing
  b. Check0
  c. Undefined
  d. Undefined

131. In mathematics, a _____ (also spelled reflexion) is a map that transforms an object into its mirror image.
  a. Reflection0
  b. Concept
  c. Undefined
  d. Undefined

132. In finance and economics, _____ is the process of finding the present value of an amount of cash at some future date, and along with compounding cash forms the basis of time value of money calculations.
  a. Thing
  b. Discount0
  c. Undefined
  d. Undefined

133. _____ is the notation in which permitted values for a variable are expressed as ranging over a certain interval; "5 < x < 9" is an example of the application of _____.
  a. Interval notation0
  b. Thing
  c. Undefined
  d. Undefined

134. _____ is a test to determine if a relation or its graph is a function or not
  a. Thing
  b. Vertical line test0
  c. Undefined
  d. Undefined

135. _____ are economic entities that give rise to future economic benefit and is controlled by the entity as a result of past transaction or other events
  a. Thing
  b. Asset0
  c. Undefined
  d. Undefined

136. _____ has many meanings, most of which simply .
  a. Power0
  b. Thing
  c. Undefined
  d. Undefined

137. _____ is the application of tools and a processing medium to the transformation of raw materials into finished goods for sale.
  a. Thing
  b. Manufacturing0
  c. Undefined
  d. Undefined

138. The _____ is a fundamental concept in analysis. Informally, a function f can be made as close to L as desired, by making x close enough to p.
  a. Thing
  b. Limit of a function0
  c. Undefined
  d. Undefined

139. In navigation, a _____ is the clockwise angle between a reference direction and the direction to an object.
   a. Bearing0
   b. Thing
   c. Undefined
   d. Undefined

140. In mathematics and logic, a _____ proof is a way of showing the truth or falsehood of a given statement by a straightforward combination of established facts, usually existing lemmas and theorems, without making any further assumptions.
   a. Thing
   b. Direct0
   c. Undefined
   d. Undefined

141. A _____ of a number is the product of that number with any integer.
   a. Multiple0
   b. Thing
   c. Undefined
   d. Undefined

142. _____ is the symbol used to indicate the nth root of a number
   a. Thing
   b. Radical0
   c. Undefined
   d. Undefined

143. A _____ is the result of the addition of a set of numbers. The numbers may be natural numbers, complex numbers, matrices, or still more complicated objects. An infinite _____ is a subtle procedure known as a series.
   a. Thing
   b. Sum0
   c. Undefined
   d. Undefined

144. In linear algebra, real numbers are called scalars and relate to vectors in a vector space through the operation of _____ multiplication, in which a vector can be multiplied by a number to produce another vector.
   a. Scalar0
   b. Thing
   c. Undefined
   d. Undefined

145. In mathematics, a _____ is an expression that is constructed from one or more variables and constants, using only the operations of addition, subtraction, multiplication, and constant positive whole number exponents. is a _____. Note in particular that division by an expression containing a variable is not in general allowed in polynomials. [1]
   a. Polynomial0
   b. Thing
   c. Undefined
   d. Undefined

146. In mathematics, the _____ (or modulus) of a real number is its numerical value without regard to its sign.
   a. Thing
   b. Absolute value0
   c. Undefined
   d. Undefined

147. In common philosophical language, a proposition or _____, is the content of an assertion, that is, it is true-or-false and defined by the meaning of a particular piece of language.
   a. Concept
   b. Statement0
   c. Undefined
   d. Undefined

148. _____ is the fee paid on borrowed money.

Chapter 2. Functions, Graphs, and Limits

a. Interest0
b. Thing
c. Undefined
d. Undefined

149. In banking and accountancy, the outstanding _____ is the amount of money owned, or due, that remains in a deposit account or a loan account at a given date, after all past remittances, payments and withdrawal have been accounted for.
a. Balance0
b. Thing
c. Undefined
d. Undefined

150. _____ interest refers to the fact that whenever interest is calculated, it is based not only on the original principal, but also on any unpaid interest that has been added to the principal.
a. Thing
b. Compound0
c. Undefined
d. Undefined

151. _____ refers to the fact that whenever interest is calculated, it is based not only on the original principal, but also on any unpaid interest that has been added to the principal. The more frequently interest is compounded, the faster the balance grows.
a. Compound interest0
b. Concept
c. Undefined
d. Undefined

152. A _____ function is a function for which, intuitively, small changes in the input result in small changes in the output.
a. Event
b. Continuous0
c. Undefined
d. Undefined

153. _____ (Groups, Algorithms and Programming) is a computer algebra system for computational discrete algebra with particular emphasis on, but not restricted to, computational group theory.
a. Thing
b. Gap0
c. Undefined
d. Undefined

154. In mathematics, a _____ number is a number which can be expressed as a ratio of two integers. Non-integer _____ numbers (commonly called fractions) are usually written as the vulgar fraction a / b, where b is not zero.
a. Thing
b. Rational0
c. Undefined
d. Undefined

155. In mathematics, a _____ is any function which can be written as the ratio of two polynomial functions.
a. Thing
b. Rational function0
c. Undefined
d. Undefined

156. In statistics, _____ means the most frequent value assumed by a random variable, or occurring in a sampling of a random variable.
a. Mode0
b. Concept
c. Undefined
d. Undefined

157. Continuous functions are of utmost importance in mathematics and applications. However, not all functions are continuous. If a function is not continuous at a point in its domain, one says that it has a _____ there. The set of all points of _____ of a function may be a discrete set, a dense set, or even the entire domain of the function.
   a. Discontinuity0
   b. Thing
   c. Undefined
   d. Undefined

158. _____ is the state of being greater than any finite real or natural number, however large.
   a. Thing
   b. Infinite0
   c. Undefined
   d. Undefined

159. A function on the real numbers is called a _____ if it can be written as a finite linear combination of indicator functions of half-open intervals.
   a. Thing
   b. Step function0
   c. Undefined
   d. Undefined

160. The _____ integers are all the integers from zero on upwards.
   a. Nonnegative0
   b. Thing
   c. Undefined
   d. Undefined

161. In mathematics, _____ is the term used for reducing the number of digits right of the decimal point, by discarding the least significant ones.
   a. Truncation0
   b. Thing
   c. Undefined
   d. Undefined

162. The population _____ is the total number of human beings alive on the planet Earth at a given time.
   a. Thing
   b. Of the world0
   c. Undefined
   d. Undefined

163. An _____ is the fee paid on borrow money.
   a. Concept
   b. Interest rate0
   c. Undefined
   d. Undefined

164. In mathematics and the mathematical sciences, a _____ is a fixed, but possibly unspecified, value. This is in contrast to a variable, which is not fixed.
   a. Constant0
   b. Thing
   c. Undefined
   d. Undefined

165. _____ are a measure of time.
   a. Thing
   b. Minutes0
   c. Undefined
   d. Undefined

166. _____ is a list of goods and materials, or those goods and materials themselves, held available in stock by a business
   a. Thing
   b. Inventory0
   c. Undefined
   d. Undefined

Chapter 2. Functions, Graphs, and Limits

167. In business, particularly accounting, a _____ is the time intervals that the accounts, statement, payments, or other calculations cover.
 a. Thing
 b. Period0
 c. Undefined
 d. Undefined

168. In abstract algebra, _____ consists of sets with binary operations that satisfy certain axioms.
 a. Thing
 b. Grouping0
 c. Undefined
 d. Undefined

169. _____ are objects, characters, or other concrete representations of ideas, concepts, or other abstractions.
 a. Thing
 b. Symbols0
 c. Undefined
 d. Undefined

170. In mathematics, _____ is an elementary arithmetic operation. When one of the numbers is a whole number, _____ is the repeated sum of the other number.
 a. Multiplication0
 b. Thing
 c. Undefined
 d. Undefined

171. In arithmetic and algebra, when a number or expression is both preceded and followed by a binary operation, an _____ is required for which operation should be applied first.
 a. Thing
 b. Order of operations0
 c. Undefined
 d. Undefined

172. In mathematics, _____ growth occurs when the growth rate of a function is always proportional to the function's current size.
 a. Exponential0
 b. Thing
 c. Undefined
 d. Undefined

173. In mathematics, a _____ is a polynomial equation of the second degree. The general form is $ax^2 + bx + c = 0$.
 a. Thing
 b. Quadratic equation0
 c. Undefined
 d. Undefined

174. A quadratic equation with real solutions, called roots, which may be real or complex, is given by the _____: $x = \frac{-b \pm \sqrt{b^2 - 4ac}}{2a}$.
 a. Thing
 b. Quadratic formula0
 c. Undefined
 d. Undefined

175. In mathematics, a _____ of a number x is a number r such that $r^2 = x$, or in words, a number r whose square (the result of multiplying the number by itself) is x.
 a. Thing
 b. Square root0
 c. Undefined
 d. Undefined

176. In mathematics, _____ is the decomposition of an object into a product of other objects, or factors, which when multiplied together give the original.

a. Thing
b. Factoring0
c. Undefined
d. Undefined

177. The existence and properties of _____ are the basis of Euclid's parallel postulate. _____ are two lines on the same plane that do not intersect even assuming that lines extend to infinity in either direction.
a. Thing
b. Parallel lines0
c. Undefined
d. Undefined

178. _____ is a state located in the southern and southwestern regions of the United States of America.
a. Texas0
b. Thing
c. Undefined
d. Undefined

179. In geometry, a _____ is defined as a quadrilateral where all four of its angles are right angles.
a. Thing
b. Rectangle0
c. Undefined
d. Undefined

180. A _____ is a first degree polynomial mathematical function of the form: f(x) = mx + b where m and b are real constants and x is a real variable.
a. Thing
b. Linear function0
c. Undefined
d. Undefined

181. In combinatorial mathematics, a _____ is an un-ordered collection of unique elements.
a. Concept
b. Combination0
c. Undefined
d. Undefined

182. In physics, _____ is an influence that may cause an object to accelerate. It may be experienced as a lift, a push, or a pull. The actual acceleration of the body is determined by the vector sum of all forces acting on it, known as net _____ or resultant _____.
a. Force0
b. Thing
c. Undefined
d. Undefined

Chapter 3. Differentiation

1. _____ are the basic objects of study in graph theory. Informally speaking, a graph is a set of objects called points, nodes, or vertices connected by links called lines or edges.
   - a. Graphs0
   - b. Thing
   - c. Undefined
   - d. Undefined

2. _____ is often used to describe the measurement of the steepness, incline, gradient, or grade of a straight line. The _____ is defined as the ratio of the "rise" divided by the "run" between two points on a line, or in other words, the ratio of the altitude change to the horizontal distance between any two points on the line.
   - a. Thing
   - b. Slope0
   - c. Undefined
   - d. Undefined

3. In trigonometry, the _____ is a function defined as $\tan x = \sin x / \cos x$. The function is so-named because it can be defined as the length of a certain segment of a _____ (in the geometric sense) to the unit circle. In plane geometry, a line is _____ to a curve, at some point, if both line and curve pass through the point with the same direction.
   - a. Tangent0
   - b. Thing
   - c. Undefined
   - d. Undefined

4. _____ has two distinct but etymologically-related meanings: one in geometry and one in trigonometry.
   - a. Thing
   - b. Tangent line0
   - c. Undefined
   - d. Undefined

5. The _____ is a measurement of how a function changes when the values of its inputs change.
   - a. Thing
   - b. Derivative0
   - c. Undefined
   - d. Undefined

6. The mathematical concept of a _____ expresses the intuitive idea of deterministic dependence between two quantities, one of which is viewed as primary and the other as secondary. A _____ then is a way to associate a unique output for each input of a specified type, for example, a real number or an element of a given set.
   - a. Function0
   - b. Thing
   - c. Undefined
   - d. Undefined

7. A _____ is a special kind of ratio, indicating a relationship between two measurements with different units, such as miles to gallons or cents to pounds.
   - a. Rate0
   - b. Thing
   - c. Undefined
   - d. Undefined

8. _____ is a mathematical subject that includes the study of limits, derivatives, integrals, and power series and constitutes a major part of modern university curriculum.
   - a. Calculus0
   - b. Thing
   - c. Undefined
   - d. Undefined

9. Sir Isaac _____, was an English physicist, mathematician, astronomer, natural philosopher, and alchemist, regarded by many as the greatest figure in the history of science
   - a. Person
   - b. Newton0
   - c. Undefined
   - d. Undefined

10. In mathematics, the concept of a _____ tries to capture the intuitive idea of a geometrical one-dimensional and continuous object. A simple example is the circle.
   a. Thing
   b. Curve0
   c. Undefined
   d. Undefined

11. Sir _____ was an English physicist, mathematician, astronomer, natural philosopher, and alchemist, regarded by many as the greatest figure in the history of science.
   a. Person
   b. Isaac Newton0
   c. Undefined
   d. Undefined

12. In Euclidean geometry, a uniform _____ is a linear transformation that enlargers or diminishes objects, and whose _____ factor is the same in all directions. This is also called homothethy.
   a. Scale0
   b. Thing
   c. Undefined
   d. Undefined

13. In mathematics, an _____, mean, or central tendency of a data set refers to a measure of the "middle" or "expected" value of the data set.
   a. Average0
   b. Concept
   c. Undefined
   d. Undefined

14. _____ is a temperature scale named after the German physicist Daniel Gabriel _____, who proposed it in 1724.
   a. Thing
   b. Fahrenheit0
   c. Undefined
   d. Undefined

15. In mathematics, there are several meanings of _____ depending on the subject.
   a. Thing
   b. Degree0
   c. Undefined
   d. Undefined

16. _____ is a physical property of a system that underlies the common notions of hot and cold; something that is hotter has the greater _____.
   a. Temperature0
   b. Thing
   c. Undefined
   d. Undefined

17. _____ is a state located in the Midwestern region of the United States of America.
   a. Minnesota0
   b. Thing
   c. Undefined
   d. Undefined

18. The _____ of measurement are a globally standardized and modernized form of the metric system.
   a. Units0
   b. Thing
   c. Undefined
   d. Undefined

19. A _____ is a numeral used to indicate a count. The most common use of the word today is to name the part of a fraction that tells the number or count of equal parts.

Chapter 3. Differentiation

a. Numerator0
b. Thing
c. Undefined
d. Undefined

20. A _____ is the part of a fraction that tells how many equal parts make up a whole, and which is used in the name of the fraction: "halves", "thirds", "fourths" or "quarters", "fifths" and so on.
    a. Denominator0
    b. Concept
    c. Undefined
    d. Undefined

21. A _____ is a symbolic representation denoting a quantity or expression. It often represents an "unknown" quantity that has the potential to change.
    a. Variable0
    b. Thing
    c. Undefined
    d. Undefined

22. In mathematics, the _____ of two sets A and B is the set that contains all elements of A that also belong to B (or equivalently, all elements of B that also belong to A), but no other elements.
    a. Intersection0
    b. Thing
    c. Undefined
    d. Undefined

23. In mathematics, a _____ is the end result of a division problem. It can also be expressed as the number of times the divisor divides into the dividend.
    a. Thing
    b. Quotient0
    c. Undefined
    d. Undefined

24. The function difference divided by the point difference is known as the _____
    a. Thing
    b. Difference quotient0
    c. Undefined
    d. Undefined

25. In mathematics, a _____ number (or a _____) is a natural number that has exactly two (distinct) natural number divisors, which are 1 and the _____ number itself.
    a. Thing
    b. Prime0
    c. Undefined
    d. Undefined

26. _____, a field in mathematics, is the study of how functions change when their inputs change. The primary object of study in _____ is the derivative.
    a. Differential calculus0
    b. Thing
    c. Undefined
    d. Undefined

27. Mathematical _____ is used to represent ideas.
    a. Notation0
    b. Thing
    c. Undefined
    d. Undefined

28. In mathematics, an _____ is any of the arguments, i.e. "inputs", to a function. Thus if we have a function f(x), then x is a _____.
    a. Independent variable0
    b. Thing
    c. Undefined
    d. Undefined

29. A _____ function is a function for which, intuitively, small changes in the input result in small changes in the output.
   a. Event
   b. Continuous0
   c. Undefined
   d. Undefined

30. Continuous functions are of utmost importance in mathematics and applications. However, not all functions are continuous. If a function is not continuous at a point in its domain, one says that it has a _____ there. The set of all points of _____ of a function may be a discrete set, a dense set, or even the entire domain of the function.
   a. Discontinuity0
   b. Thing
   c. Undefined
   d. Undefined

31. In mathematics, a _____ of a k-place relation $L \subseteq X_1 \times \ldots \times X_k$ is one of the sets X_j, $1 \le j \le k$. In the special case where k = 2 and $L \subseteq X_1 \times X_2$ is a function $L : X_1 \to X_2$, it is conventional to refer to X_1 as the _____ of the function and to refer to X_2 as the codomain of the function.
   a. Thing
   b. Domain0
   c. Undefined
   d. Undefined

32. A _____ is an individual or household that purchases and uses goods and services generated within the economy.
   a. Thing
   b. Consumer0
   c. Undefined
   d. Undefined

33. In business, particularly accounting, a _____ is the time intervals that the accounts, statement, payments, or other calculations cover.
   a. Period0
   b. Thing
   c. Undefined
   d. Undefined

34. _____ is a business term for the amount of money that a company receives from its activities in a given period, mostly from sales of products and/or services to customers
   a. Thing
   b. Revenue0
   c. Undefined
   d. Undefined

35. In elementary algebra, an _____ is a set that contains every real number between two indicated numbers and may contain the two numbers themselves.
   a. Thing
   b. Interval0
   c. Undefined
   d. Undefined

36. In mathematics, the _____ f is the collection of all ordered pairs . In particular, graph means the graphical representation of this collection, in the form of a curve or surface, together with axes, etc. Graphing on a Cartesian plane is sometimes referred to as curve sketching.
   a. Thing
   b. Graph of a function0
   c. Undefined
   d. Undefined

37. In mathematics and the mathematical sciences, a _____ is a fixed, but possibly unspecified, value. This is in contrast to a variable, which is not fixed.

Chapter 3. Differentiation

a. Constant0
b. Thing
c. Undefined
d. Undefined

38. An _____ of a product of sums expresses it as a sum of products by using the fact that multiplication distributes over addition.
    a. Expansion0
    b. Thing
    c. Undefined
    d. Undefined

39. _____ has many meanings, most of which simply .
    a. Power0
    b. Thing
    c. Undefined
    d. Undefined

40. _____ is a method for differentiating expressions involving exponentiation the power operation.
    a. Thing
    b. Power rule0
    c. Undefined
    d. Undefined

41. In elementary algebra, a _____ is a polynomial with two terms: the sum of two monomials. It is the simplest kind of polynomial except for a monomial.
    a. Thing
    b. Binomial0
    c. Undefined
    d. Undefined

42. In mathematics, a _____ may be described informally as a number that can be given by an infinite decimal representation.
    a. Thing
    b. Real number0
    c. Undefined
    d. Undefined

43. In mathematics, a _____ is a demonstration that, assuming certain axioms, some statement is necessarily true.
    a. Thing
    b. Proof0
    c. Undefined
    d. Undefined

44. A _____ of a number is the product of that number with any integer.
    a. Thing
    b. Multiple0
    c. Undefined
    d. Undefined

45. _____, either of the curved-bracket punctuation marks that together make a set of _____
    a. Thing
    b. Parentheses0
    c. Undefined
    d. Undefined

46. In mathematical logic, a Gödel numbering (or Gödel _____) is a function that assigns to each symbol and well-formed formula of some formal language a unique natural number called its Gödel number.
    a. Thing
    b. Code0
    c. Undefined
    d. Undefined

47. In mathematics, a _____ number is a number which can be expressed as a ratio of two integers. Non-integer _____ numbers (commonly called fractions) are usually written as the vulgar fraction a / b, where b is not zero.

a. Thing
b. Rational0
c. Undefined
d. Undefined

48. _____ is a mathematical operation, written a^n, involving two numbers, the base a and the exponent n.
a. Thing
b. Exponentiating0
c. Undefined
d. Undefined

49. _____ is a mathematical operation, written a^n, involving two numbers, the base a and the exponent n.
a. Exponentiation0
b. Thing
c. Undefined
d. Undefined

50. _____ is a branch of mathematics concerning the study of structure, relation and quantity.
a. Algebra0
b. Concept
c. Undefined
d. Undefined

51. _____ is the symbold used to indicate the nth root of a number
a. Radical0
b. Thing
c. Undefined
d. Undefined

52. A _____ is the result of the addition of a set of numbers. The numbers may be natural numbers, complex numbers, matrices, or still more complicated objects. An infinite _____ is a subtle procedure known as a series.
a. Thing
b. Sum0
c. Undefined
d. Undefined

53. In mathematics, a set is called _____ if there is a bijection between the set and some set of the form {1, 2, ..., n} where n is a natural number.
a. Thing
b. Finite0
c. Undefined
d. Undefined

54. In sociology and biology a _____ is the collection of people or organisms of a particular species living in a given geographic area or space, usually measured by a census.
a. Population0
b. Thing
c. Undefined
d. Undefined

55. An _____ is a combination of numbers, operators, grouping symbols and/or free variables and bound variables arranged in a meaningful way which can be evaluated..
a. Thing
b. Expression0
c. Undefined
d. Undefined

56. In astronomy, geography, geometry and related sciences and contexts, a plane is said to be _____ at a given point if it is locally perpendicular to the gradient of the gravity field, i.e., with the direction of the gravitational force at that point.
a. Thing
b. Horizontal0
c. Undefined
d. Undefined

57. A _____ is a set of numbers that designate location in a given reference system, such as x,y in a planar _____ system or an x,y,z in a three-dimensional _____ system.

Chapter 3. Differentiation

    a. Coordinate0
    b. Thing
    c. Undefined
    d. Undefined

58. An _____ is when two lines intersect somewhere on a plane creating a right angle at intersection
    a. Axes0
    b. Thing
    c. Undefined
    d. Undefined

59. _____ is the application of tools and a processing medium to the transformation of raw materials into finished goods for sale.
    a. Thing
    b. Manufacturing0
    c. Undefined
    d. Undefined

60. In mathematics, in the field of group theory, a _____ of a group is a quasisimple subnormal subgroup.
    a. Component0
    b. Concept
    c. Undefined
    d. Undefined

61. Fixed costs are expenses whose total does not change in proportion to the activity of a business.Unit fixed costs decline with volume following a retangular hyperbola as the volume of production.Variable costs by contrast change in relation to the activity of a business such as sales or production volume.Along with variable costs,fixed costs make up one of the two components of total cost. In the most simple production function total cost is equal to fixed costs plus variable costs.In accounting terminology, fixed costs will broadly include all costs which are not included in cost of goods sold, and variable costs are those captured in costs of goods sold. The implicit assumption required to make the equivalence between the accounting and economics terminology is that the accounting period is equal to the period in which fixed costs do not vary in relation to production. In practice, this equivalence does not always hold and depending on the period under consideration by management, some overhead expenses can be adjusted by management, and the specific allocation of each expense to each category will be decided under cost accounting.In business planning and management accounting, usage of the terms fixed costs, variable costs and others will often differ from usage in economics, and may depend on the intended use. For example, costs may be segregated into per unit costs fixed costs per period, and variable costs as a proportion of revenue. Capital expenditures will usually be allocated separately, and depending on the purpose, a portion may be regularly allocated to expenses as depreciation and amortization and seen as a _____ per period, or the entire amount may be considered upfront fixed costs.
    a. Thing
    b. Fixed cost0
    c. Undefined
    d. Undefined

62. _____, from Latin meaning "to make progress", is defined in two different ways. Pure economic _____ is the increase in wealth that an investor has from making an investment, taking into consideration all costs associated with that investment including the opportunity cost of capital.
    a. Profit0
    b. Thing
    c. Undefined
    d. Undefined

63. The _____ (symbol _____) and the millibar (symbol mbar, also mb) are units of pressure.
    a. Thing
    b. Bar0
    c. Undefined
    d. Undefined

64. _____ are expenses whose total does not change in proportion to the activity of a business, within the relevant time period or scale of production

Chapter 3. Differentiation

a. Fixed costs0   b. Thing
c. Undefined   d. Undefined

65. The deductive-nomological model is a formalized view of scientific _____ in natural language.
    a. Thing   b. Explanation0
    c. Undefined   d. Undefined

66. In common philosophical language, a proposition or _____, is the content of an assertion, that is, it is true-or-false and defined by the meaning of a particular piece of language.
    a. Statement0   b. Concept
    c. Undefined   d. Undefined

67. _____ of an object is its speed in a particular direction.
    a. Thing   b. Velocity0
    c. Undefined   d. Undefined

68. In mathematics, a _____ is the result of multiplying, or an expression that identifies factors to be multiplied.
    a. Product0   b. Thing
    c. Undefined   d. Undefined

69. _____ is the change in total cost that arises when the quantity produced changes by one unit.
    a. Thing   b. Marginal cost0
    c. Undefined   d. Undefined

70. _____ is the extra revenue that an additional unit of product will bring a firm. It can also be described as the change in total revenue/change in number of units sold.
    a. Marginal revenue0   b. Thing
    c. Undefined   d. Undefined

71. _____ is change in population over time, and can be quantified as the change in the number of individuals in a population per unit time.
    a. Population growth0   b. Thing
    c. Undefined   d. Undefined

72. _____ is defined as the rate of change or derivative with respect to time of velocity.
    a. Thing   b. Acceleration0
    c. Undefined   d. Undefined

73. _____ the expected value of a random variable displays the average or central value of the variable. It is a summary value of the distribution of the variable.
    a. Determining0   b. Thing
    c. Undefined   d. Undefined

74. _____ is a trigonometric function that is the reciprocal of cosine.

a. Secant0
b. Thing
c. Undefined
d. Undefined

75. _____ of a curve is a line that intersects two or more points on the curve.
   a. Secant line0
   b. Thing
   c. Undefined
   d. Undefined

76. In geometry, an _____ is a point at which a line segment or ray terminates.
   a. Thing
   b. Endpoint0
   c. Undefined
   d. Undefined

77. _____ are a measure of time.
   a. Thing
   b. Minutes0
   c. Undefined
   d. Undefined

78. Initial objects are also called _____, and terminal objects are also called final.
   a. Coterminal0
   b. Thing
   c. Undefined
   d. Undefined

79. In mathematics, the _____ (or modulus) of a real number is its numerical value without regard to its sign.
   a. Thing
   b. Absolute value0
   c. Undefined
   d. Undefined

80. _____ is the largest positive integer that divides both numbers without remainder.
   a. Thing
   b. Common Factor0
   c. Undefined
   d. Undefined

81. The word _____ comes from the 15th Century Latin word discretus which means separate.
   a. Thing
   b. Discrete0
   c. Undefined
   d. Undefined

82. In economics, supply and _____ describe market relations between prospective sellers and buyers of a good.
   a. Demand0
   b. Thing
   c. Undefined
   d. Undefined

83. In mathematics, _____ refers to the rewriting of an expression into a simpler form.
   a. Reduction0
   b. Thing
   c. Undefined
   d. Undefined

84. A _____ is 360° or 2δ radians.
   a. Thing
   b. Turn0
   c. Undefined
   d. Undefined

85. _____ is a synonym for information.

a. Thing
b. Data0
c. Undefined
d. Undefined

86. Equivalence is the condition of being _____ or essentially equal.
a. Thing
b. Equivalent0
c. Undefined
d. Undefined

87. _____ element of an element x with respect to a binary operation * with identity element e is an element y such that x * y = y * x = e. In particular,
a. Inverse0
b. Thing
c. Undefined
d. Undefined

88. An _____ is a function which does the reverse of a given function.
a. Inverse function0
b. Thing
c. Undefined
d. Undefined

89. _____ is a kind of property which exists as magnitude or multitude. It is among the basic classes of things along with quality, substance, change, and relation.
a. Amount0
b. Thing
c. Undefined
d. Undefined

90. In mathematics, a _____ is a countable collection of open covers of a topological space that satisfies certain separation axioms.
a. Development0
b. Thing
c. Undefined
d. Undefined

91. In plane geometry, a _____ is a polygon with four equal sides, four right angles, and parallel opposite sides. In algebra, the _____ of a number is that number multiplied by itself.
a. Square0
b. Thing
c. Undefined
d. Undefined

92. _____ is a term applied when talking about the movement of air from one place to the next.
a. Wind speed0
b. Thing
c. Undefined
d. Undefined

93. _____ is, or relates to, the _____ temperature scale .
a. Thing
b. Celsius0
c. Undefined
d. Undefined

94. The metre (or _____, see spelling differences) is a measure of length. It is the basic unit of length in the metric system and in the International System of Units (SI), used around the world for general and scientific purposes.
a. Meter0
b. Concept
c. Undefined
d. Undefined

95. _____ is the transport of people on a trip/journey or the process or time involved in a person or object moving from one location to another.

Chapter 3. Differentiation

a. Thing
b. Travel0
c. Undefined
d. Undefined

96. A _____ is a unit of length in the metric system, equal to one thousand metres, the current SI base unit of length
   a. Kilometer0
   b. Thing
   c. Undefined
   d. Undefined

97. _____, Greek for "knowledge of nature," is the branch of science concerned with the discovery and characterization of universal laws which govern matter, energy, space, and time.
   a. Physics0
   b. Thing
   c. Undefined
   d. Undefined

98. _____ is the level of functional and/or metabolic efficiency of an organism at both the micro level.
   a. Thing
   b. Health0
   c. Undefined
   d. Undefined

99. The word _____ comes from the Latin word linearis, which means created by lines.
   a. Linear0
   b. Thing
   c. Undefined
   d. Undefined

100. _____ is a list of goods and materials, or those goods and materials themselves, held available in stock by a business
   a. Inventory0
   b. Thing
   c. Undefined
   d. Undefined

101. In geometry, the _____ of an object is a point in some sense in the middle of the object.
   a. Center0
   b. Thing
   c. Undefined
   d. Undefined

102. A _____ is a unit of length, usually used to measure distance, in a number of different systems, including Imperial units, United States customary units and Norwegian/Swedish mil. Its size can vary from system to system, but in each is between 1 and 10 kilometers. In contemporary English contexts _____ refers to either:
   a. Mile0
   b. Thing
   c. Undefined
   d. Undefined

103. The _____ governs the differentiation of products of differentiable functions.
   a. Thing
   b. Product rule0
   c. Undefined
   d. Undefined

104. The _____ is a method of finding the derivative of a function that is the quotient of two other functions for which derivatives exist.
   a. Thing
   b. Quotient rule0
   c. Undefined
   d. Undefined

105. In economics, economic _____ is simply a state of the world where economic forces are balanced and in the absence of external influences the values of economic variables will not change.

a. Thing
b. Equilibrium0
c. Undefined
d. Undefined

106. Mathematical _____ are demonstrations that,assuming certain axioms, some statement is necessarily true.
a. Proofs0
b. Thing
c. Undefined
d. Undefined

107. In calculus, the _____ in differentiation is a method of finding the derivative of a function that is the sum of two other functions for which derivatives exist.
a. Thing
b. Sum Rule0
c. Undefined
d. Undefined

108. In mathematics, factorization (British English: factorisation) or factoring is the decomposition of an object (for example, a number, a polynomial, or a matrix) into a product of other objects, or _____, which when multiplied together give the original.
a. Thing
b. Factors0
c. Undefined
d. Undefined

109. In mathematics, a _____ is an expression that is constructed from one or more variables and constants, using only the operations of addition, subtraction, multiplication, and constant positive whole number exponents. is a _____. Note in particular that division by an expression containing a variable is not in general allowed in polynomials. [1]
a. Polynomial0
b. Thing
c. Undefined
d. Undefined

110. In mathematics, a _____ is any function which can be written as the ratio of two polynomial functions.
a. Rational function0
b. Thing
c. Undefined
d. Undefined

111. The plus and _____ signs are mathematical symbols used to represent the notions of positive and negative as well as the operations of addition and subtraction.
a. Thing
b. Minus0
c. Undefined
d. Undefined

112. In mathematics, _____ expressions is used to reduce the expression into the lowest possible term.
a. Simplifying0
b. Thing
c. Undefined
d. Undefined

113. In mathematics and logic, a _____ proof is a way of showing the truth or falsehood of a given statement by a straightforward combination of established facts, usually existing lemmas and theorems, without making any further assumptions.
a. Direct0
b. Thing
c. Undefined
d. Undefined

114. A _____ is a function that assigns a number to subsets of a given set.

Chapter 3. Differentiation

  a. Measure0
  b. Thing
  c. Undefined
  d. Undefined

115. _____ is a way of expressing a number as a fraction of 100 per cent meaning "per hundred".
  a. Thing
  b. Percent0
  c. Undefined
  d. Undefined

116. _____ consists of the knowledge of various products to protect the public from fraudulent or unforseeable circumstances.
  a. Consumer awareness0
  b. Thing
  c. Undefined
  d. Undefined

117. Deductive _____ is the kind of _____ in which the conclusion is necessitated by, or reached from, previously known facts (the premises).
  a. Thing
  b. Reasoning0
  c. Undefined
  d. Undefined

118. Transport or _____ is the movement of people and goods from one place to another.
  a. Thing
  b. Transportation0
  c. Undefined
  d. Undefined

119. Order theory is a branch of mathematics that studies various kinds of binary relations that capture the intuitive notion of a mathematical _____.
  a. Thing
  b. Ordering0
  c. Undefined
  d. Undefined

120. A frame of _____ is a particular perspective from which the universe is observed.
  a. Reference0
  b. Thing
  c. Undefined
  d. Undefined

121. In calculus, the _____ is a formula for the derivative of the composite of two functions.
  a. Chain rule0
  b. Concept
  c. Undefined
  d. Undefined

122. _____ is informally a function which satisfies a polynomial equation whose coefficients are themselves polynomials.
  a. Thing
  b. Algebraic function0
  c. Undefined
  d. Undefined

123. In mathematics, a _____ of a positive integer n is a way of writing n as a sum of positive integers.
  a. Thing
  b. Composition0
  c. Undefined
  d. Undefined

124. The _____ functions is determined by the nesting of two or more functions to form a single new function.

a. Composition of two0
b. Thing
c. Undefined
d. Undefined

125. A _____ number is a positive integer which has a positive divisor other than one or itself.
    a. Composite0
    b. Thing
    c. Undefined
    d. Undefined

126. A _____, formed by the composition of one function on another, represents the application of the former to the result of the application of the latter to the argument of the composite.
    a. Composite function0
    b. Thing
    c. Undefined
    d. Undefined

127. In mathematics, _____ is the decomposition of an object into a product of other objects, or factors, which when multiplied together give the original.
    a. Thing
    b. Factoring0
    c. Undefined
    d. Undefined

128. In Graph theory, a _____ is a digraph with weighted edges.
    a. Concept
    b. Network0
    c. Undefined
    d. Undefined

129. A _____ is a negotiable instrument instructing a financial institution to pay a specific amount of a specific currency from a specific demand account held in the maker/depositor's name with that institution. Both the maker and payee may be natural persons or legal entities.
    a. Thing
    b. Check0
    c. Undefined
    d. Undefined

130. _____ is the fee paid on borrowed money.
    a. Thing
    b. Interest0
    c. Undefined
    d. Undefined

131. _____ interest refers to the fact that whenever interest is calculated, it is based not only on the original principal, but also on any unpaid interest that has been added to the principal.
    a. Compound0
    b. Thing
    c. Undefined
    d. Undefined

132. _____ refers to the fact that whenever interest is calculated, it is based not only on the original principal, but also on any unpaid interest that has been added to the principal. The more frequently interest is compounded, the faster the balance grows.
    a. Compound interest0
    b. Concept
    c. Undefined
    d. Undefined

133. An _____ is the fee paid on borrow money.
    a. Concept
    b. Interest rate0
    c. Undefined
    d. Undefined

Chapter 3. Differentiation

134. In banking and accountancy, the outstanding _____ is the amount of money owned, or due, that remains in a deposit account or a loan account at a given date, after all past remittances, payments and withdrawal have been accounted for.
 a. Thing
 b. Balance0
 c. Undefined
 d. Undefined

135. In mathematics, two quantities are called _____ if they vary in such a way that one of the quantities is a constant multiple of the other, or equivalently if they have a constant ratio.
 a. Proportional0
 b. Thing
 c. Undefined
 d. Undefined

136. In mathematics, a _____ of a number x is a number r such that $r^2 = x$, or in words, a number r whose square (the result of multiplying the number by itself) is x.
 a. Thing
 b. Square root0
 c. Undefined
 d. Undefined

137. In mathematics, a _____ of a complex-valued function f is a member x of the domain of f such that f(x) vanishes at x, that is, x : f (x) = 0.
 a. Thing
 b. Root0
 c. Undefined
 d. Undefined

138. _____ is a term used in accounting, economics and finance with reference to the fact that assets with finite lives lose value over time.
 a. Thing
 b. Depreciation0
 c. Undefined
 d. Undefined

139. A _____ is a system of payment named after the small plastic card issued to users of the system.
 a. Credit card0
 b. Thing
 c. Undefined
 d. Undefined

140. A _____ is a three-dimensional solid object bounded by six square faces, facets, or sides, with three meeting at each vertex.
 a. Cube0
 b. Thing
 c. Undefined
 d. Undefined

141. A _____ of a number is a number a such that $a^3 = x$.
 a. Thing
 b. Cube root0
 c. Undefined
 d. Undefined

142. In linear algebra, the _____ of an n-by-n square matrix A is defined to be the sum of the elements on the main diagonal of A,
 a. Trace0
 b. Thing
 c. Undefined
 d. Undefined

143. In geographic information systems, a _____ comprises an entity with a geographic location, typically determined by points, arcs, or polygons. Carriageways and cadastres exemplify _____ data.

a. Feature0   b. Thing
c. Undefined   d. Undefined

144. _____ studies and addresses the ways in which individuals, businesses, and organizations raise, allocate, and use monetary resources over time, taking into account the risks entailed in their projects
a. Finance0   b. Thing
c. Undefined   d. Undefined

145. In mathematics, a _____ case is a limiting case in which a class of object changes its nature so as to belong to another, usually simpler, class.
a. Thing   b. Degenerate0
c. Undefined   d. Undefined

146. _____ is a function whose values do not vary and thus are constant.
a. Constant function0   b. Thing
c. Undefined   d. Undefined

147. The _____ of a ring R is defined to be the smallest positive integer n such that $n\,a = 0$, for all a in R.
a. Thing   b. Characteristic0
c. Undefined   d. Undefined

148. A _____, as defined by the International Astronomical Union, is a celestial body orbiting a star or stellar remnant that is massive enough to be rounded by its own gravity, not massive enough to cause thermonuclear fusion in its core, and has cleared its neighboring region of planetesimals.
a. Thing   b. Planet0
c. Undefined   d. Undefined

149. The _____ or kilogramme is the SI base unit of mass. It is defined as being equal to the mass of the international prototype of the _____.
a. Kilogram0   b. Thing
c. Undefined   d. Undefined

150. In classical geometry, a _____ of a circle or sphere is any line segment from its center to its boundary. By extension, the _____ of a circle or sphere is the length of any such segment. The _____ is half the diameter. In science and engineering the term _____ of curvature is commonly used as a synonym for _____.
a. Thing   b. Radius0
c. Undefined   d. Undefined

151. _____ is the property of a physical object that quantifies the amount of matter and energy it is equivalent to.
a. Thing   b. Mass0
c. Undefined   d. Undefined

152. A _____ is a quantity that denotes the proportional amount or magnitude of one quantity relative to another.
a. Thing   b. Ratio0
c. Undefined   d. Undefined

Chapter 3. Differentiation

153. In mathematics, the _____ of a function is the set of all "output" values produced by that function. Given a function $f : A \to B$, the _____ of f, is defined to be the set $\{x \in B : x = f(a) \text{ for some } a \in A\}$.
   a. Thing
   b. Range0
   c. Undefined
   d. Undefined

154. _____ is a unit of speed, expressing the number of international miles covered per hour.
   a. Thing
   b. Miles per hour0
   c. Undefined
   d. Undefined

155. A _____ is any object propelled through space by the applicationp of a force.
   a. Projectile0
   b. Thing
   c. Undefined
   d. Undefined

156. _____ is the path a moving object follows through space.
   a. Projectile motion0
   b. Thing
   c. Undefined
   d. Undefined

157. _____ is to give an equation $R(x,y) = S(x,y)$ that at least in part has the same graph as $y = f(x)$.
   a. Thing
   b. Implicit differentiation0
   c. Undefined
   d. Undefined

158. In Euclidean geometry, a _____ is the set of all points in a plane at a fixed distance, called the radius, from a given point, the center.
   a. Thing
   b. Circle0
   c. Undefined
   d. Undefined

159. In mathematics, an _____ .
   a. Thing
   b. Ellipse0
   c. Undefined
   d. Undefined

160. _____ asserts that the maximum output of a technologically-determined production process is a mathematical function of input factors of production.
   a. Thing
   b. Production function0
   c. Undefined
   d. Undefined

161. In epidemiology, an _____ is a disease that appears as new cases in a given human population, during a given period, at a rate that substantially exceeds with is "expected," based on recent experience.
   a. Thing
   b. Epidemic0
   c. Undefined
   d. Undefined

162. In differential calculus, _____ problems involve finding the rate at which a quantity is changing by relating that quantity to other quantities whose rates of change are known.
   a. Related rates0
   b. Thing
   c. Undefined
   d. Undefined

Chapter 3. Differentiation

163. A _____ is an abstract model that uses mathematical language to describe the behavior of a system. Eykhoff defined a _____ as 'a representation of the essential aspects of an existing system which presents knowledge of that system in usable form'.
   a. Mathematical model0
   b. Thing
   c. Undefined
   d. Undefined

164. _____ are any documents that aim to streamline particular processes according to a set routine.
   a. Thing
   b. Guidelines0
   c. Undefined
   d. Undefined

165. The _____ of a solid object is the three-dimensional concept of how much space it occupies, often quantified numerically.
   a. Thing
   b. Volume0
   c. Undefined
   d. Undefined

166. In mathematics, a _____ is the set of all points in three-dimensional space (R^3) which are at distance r from a fixed point of that space, where r is a positive real number called the radius of the _____. The fixed point is called the center or centre, and is not part of the _____ itself.
   a. Sphere0
   b. Thing
   c. Undefined
   d. Undefined

167. A _____ is one of the basic shapes of geometry: a polygon with three vertices and three sides which are straight line segments.
   a. Triangle0
   b. Thing
   c. Undefined
   d. Undefined

168. _____ is a three-dimensional geometric shape formed by straight lines through a fixed point vertex to the points of a fixed curve directrix.
   a. Thing
   b. Right circular cone0
   c. Undefined
   d. Undefined

169. A _____ is a three-dimensional geometric shape formed by straight lines through a fixed point (vertex) to the points of a fixed curve (directrix)
   a. Cone0
   b. Concept
   c. Undefined
   d. Undefined

170. In geometry and trigonometry, a _____ is defined as an angle between two straight intersecting lines of ninety degrees, or one-quarter of a circle.
   a. Thing
   b. Right angle0
   c. Undefined
   d. Undefined

171. In geometry, an _____ of a triangle is a straight line through a vertex and perpendicular to (i.e. forming a right angle with) the opposite side or an extension of the opposite side.
   a. Altitude0
   b. Concept
   c. Undefined
   d. Undefined

Chapter 3. Differentiation

172. _____ is a service provided by ground-based controllers who direct aircraft on the ground and in the air.
 a. Thing
 b. Air traffic control0
 c. Undefined
 d. Undefined

173. In mathematics, _____ are used to indicate the square root of a number.
 a. Thing
 b. Radicals0
 c. Undefined
 d. Undefined

174. In geometry, a _____ (Greek words diairo = divide and metro = measure) of a circle is any straight line segment that passes through the centre and whose endpoints are on the circular boundary, or, in more modern usage, the length of such a line segment. When using the word in the more modern sense, one speaks of the _____ rather than a _____, because all diameters of a circle have the same length. This length is twice the radius. The _____ of a circle is also the longest chord that the circle has.
 a. Thing
 b. Diameter0
 c. Undefined
 d. Undefined

175. _____ is the art, science, and practice of studying and managing forests and plantations, and related natural resources.
 a. Thing
 b. Forestry0
 c. Undefined
 d. Undefined

Chapter 4. Applications of the Derivative

1. The mathematical concept of a _____ expresses the intuitive idea of deterministic dependence between two quantities, one of which is viewed as primary and the other as secondary. A _____ then is a way to associate a unique output for each input of a specified type, for example, a real number or an element of a given set.
   a. Function0
   b. Thing
   c. Undefined
   d. Undefined

2. In elementary algebra, an _____ is a set that contains every real number between two indicated numbers and may contain the two numbers themselves.
   a. Interval0
   b. Thing
   c. Undefined
   d. Undefined

3. The _____ is a measurement of how a function changes when the values of its inputs change.
   a. Derivative0
   b. Thing
   c. Undefined
   d. Undefined

4. In statistics, a _____ measure is one which is measuring what is supposed to measure.
   a. Valid0
   b. Thing
   c. Undefined
   d. Undefined

5. Acid _____ ratio measures the ability of a company to use its near cash or quick assets to immediately extinguish its current liabilities.
   a. Thing
   b. Test0
   c. Undefined
   d. Undefined

6. In a mathematical proof or a syllogism, a _____ is a statement that is the logical consequence of preceding statements.
   a. Conclusion0
   b. Concept
   c. Undefined
   d. Undefined

7. In mathematics and the mathematical sciences, a _____ is a fixed, but possibly unspecified, value. This is in contrast to a variable, which is not fixed.
   a. Thing
   b. Constant0
   c. Undefined
   d. Undefined

8. In mathematics, a set is called _____ if there is a bijection between the set and some set of the form {1, 2, ..., n} where n is a natural number.
   a. Thing
   b. Finite0
   c. Undefined
   d. Undefined

9. In mathematics, defined and _____ are used to explain whether or not expressions have meaningful, sensible, and unambiguous values.
   a. Undefined0
   b. Thing
   c. Undefined
   d. Undefined

10. In mathematics, a _____ of a k-place relation $L \subseteq X_1 \times ... \times X_k$ is one of the sets X_j, $1 \leq j \leq k$. In the special case where k = 2 and $L \subseteq X_1 \times X_2$ is a function $L : X_1 \rightarrow X_2$, it is conventional to refer to X_1 as the _____ of the function and to refer to X_2 as the codomain of the function.

Chapter 4. Applications of the Derivative

a. Thing
b. Domain0
c. Undefined
d. Undefined

11. A _____ function is a function for which, intuitively, small changes in the input result in small changes in the output.
a. Event
b. Continuous0
c. Undefined
d. Undefined

12. _____ are any documents that aim to streamline particular processes according to a set routine.
a. Guidelines0 .
b. Thing
c. Undefined
d. Undefined

13. _____ is a business term for the amount of money that a company receives from its activities in a given period, mostly from sales of products and/or services to customers
a. Revenue0
b. Thing
c. Undefined
d. Undefined

14. _____, from Latin meaning "to make progress", is defined in two different ways. Pure economic _____ is the increase in wealth that an investor has from making an investment, taking into consideration all costs associated with that investment including the opportunity cost of capital.
a. Profit0
b. Thing
c. Undefined
d. Undefined

15. _____ are the basic objects of study in graph theory. Informally speaking, a graph is a set of objects called points, nodes, or vertices connected by links called lines or edges.
a. Thing
b. Graphs0
c. Undefined
d. Undefined

16. An _____ is a combination of numbers, operators, grouping symbols and/or free variables and bound variables arranged in a meaningful way which can be evaluated..
a. Thing
b. Expression0
c. Undefined
d. Undefined

17. _____ of an object is its speed in a particular direction.
a. Thing
b. Velocity0
c. Undefined
d. Undefined

18. In mathematics, there are several meanings of _____ depending on the subject.
a. Degree0
b. Thing
c. Undefined
d. Undefined

19. _____ is a physical property of a system that underlies the common notions of hot and cold; something that is hotter has the greater _____.
a. Thing
b. Temperature0
c. Undefined
d. Undefined

Chapter 4. Applications of the Derivative

20. The metre (or _____, see spelling differences) is a measure of length. It is the basic unit of length in the metric system and in the International System of Units (SI), used around the world for general and scientific purposes.
    a. Meter0   b. Concept
    c. Undefined   d. Undefined

21. Transport or _____ is the movement of people and goods from one place to another.
    a. Thing   b. Transportation0
    c. Undefined   d. Undefined

22. Order theory is a branch of mathematics that studies various kinds of binary relations that capture the intuitive notion of a mathematical _____.
    a. Ordering0   b. Thing
    c. Undefined   d. Undefined

23. in mathematics, maxima and minima, known collectively as _____, are the largest value maximum or smallest value minimum, that a function takes in a point either within a given neighborhood or on the function domain in its entirety global extremum.
    a. Extrema0   b. Thing
    c. Undefined   d. Undefined

24. The term _____ refers to the largest and the smallest element of a set.
    a. Extreme value0   b. Thing
    c. Undefined   d. Undefined

25. In mathematics, maxima and minima, known collectively as extrema, are the largest value maximum or smallest value minimum, that a function takes in a point either within a given neighborhood local _____ or on the function domain in its entirety global _____.
    a. Thing   b. Extremum0
    c. Undefined   d. Undefined

26. _____ is a free computer algebra system based on a 1982 version of Macsyma
    a. Thing   b. Maxima0
    c. Undefined   d. Undefined

27. In mathematics, maxima and _____, known collectively as extrema, are points in the domain of a function at which the function takes a largest value .
    a. Minima0   b. Thing
    c. Undefined   d. Undefined

28. The _____ is the highest point in a certain portion of a graph.
    a. Relative maximum0   b. Thing
    c. Undefined   d. Undefined

29. The _____ is the lowest point in a certain portion of a graph.

Chapter 4. Applications of the Derivative

a. Thing
b. Relative minimum0
c. Undefined
d. Undefined

30. In linear algebra, the _____ of an n-by-n square matrix A is defined to be the sum of the elements on the main diagonal of A,
    a. Thing
    b. Trace0
    c. Undefined
    d. Undefined

31. In geographic information systems, a _____ comprises an entity with a geographic location, typically determined by points, arcs, or polygons. Carriageways and cadastres exemplify _____ data.
    a. Thing
    b. Feature0
    c. Undefined
    d. Undefined

32. _____, a field in mathematics, is the study of how functions change when their inputs change. The primary object of study in _____ is the derivative.
    a. Differential calculus0
    b. Thing
    c. Undefined
    d. Undefined

33. In mathematics, a _____ is a statement that can be proved on the basis of explicitly stated or previously agreed assumptions.
    a. Thing
    b. Theorem0
    c. Undefined
    d. Undefined

34. In geometry, an _____ is a point at which a line segment or ray terminates.
    a. Endpoint0
    b. Thing
    c. Undefined
    d. Undefined

35. _____ is a mathematical subject that includes the study of limits, derivatives, integrals, and power series and constitutes a major part of modern university curriculum.
    a. Calculus0
    b. Thing
    c. Undefined
    d. Undefined

36. The _____ of measurement are a globally standardized and modernized form of the metric system.
    a. Thing
    b. Units0
    c. Undefined
    d. Undefined

37. A _____ is 360° or 2δ radians.
    a. Turn0
    b. Thing
    c. Undefined
    d. Undefined

38. In mathematics, a _____ is the result of multiplying, or an expression that identifies factors to be multiplied.
    a. Product0
    b. Thing
    c. Undefined
    d. Undefined

39. In mathematics, two quantities are called _____ if they vary in such a way that one of the quantities is a constant multiple of the other, or equivalently if they have a constant ratio.

Chapter 4. Applications of the Derivative

    a. Thing
    b. Proportional0
    c. Undefined
    d. Undefined

40. A _____ is a three-dimensional solid object bounded by six square faces, facets, or sides, with three meeting at each vertex.
    a. Cube0
    b. Thing
    c. Undefined
    d. Undefined

41. In classical geometry, a _____ of a circle or sphere is any line segment from its center to its boundary. By extension, the _____ of a circle or sphere is the length of any such segment. The _____ is half the diameter. In science and engineering the term _____ of curvature is commonly used as a synonym for _____.
    a. Radius0
    b. Thing
    c. Undefined
    d. Undefined

42. A _____ is a quantity that denotes the proportional amount or magnitude of one quantity relative to another.
    a. Thing
    b. Ratio0
    c. Undefined
    d. Undefined

43. _____ refers to selected population characteristics as used in government, marketing or opinion research, or the demographic profiles used in such research.
    a. Demographics0
    b. Thing
    c. Undefined
    d. Undefined

44. A _____ is a special kind of ratio, indicating a relationship between two measurements with different units, such as miles to gallons or cents to pounds.
    a. Rate0
    b. Thing
    c. Undefined
    d. Undefined

45. The word _____ means curving in or hollowed inward.
    a. Concavity0
    b. Thing
    c. Undefined
    d. Undefined

46. _____ the expected value of a random variable displays the average or central value of the variable. It is a summary value of the distribution of the variable.
    a. Thing
    b. Determining0
    c. Undefined
    d. Undefined

47. In trigonometry, the _____ is a function defined as $\tan x = \sin x / \cos x$. The function is so-named because it can be defined as the length of a certain segment of a _____ (in the geometric sense) to the unit circle. In plane geometry, a line is _____ to a curve, at some point, if both line and curve pass through the point with the same direction.
    a. Tangent0
    b. Thing
    c. Undefined
    d. Undefined

48. _____ has two distinct but etymologically-related meanings: one in geometry and one in trigonometry.

Chapter 4. Applications of the Derivative

    a. Tangent line0
    c. Undefined
    b. Thing
    d. Undefined

49. In mathematics, the concept of a _____ tries to capture the intuitive idea of a geometrical one-dimensional and continuous object. A simple example is the circle.
    a. Thing
    c. Undefined
    b. Curve0
    d. Undefined

50. Continuous functions are of utmost importance in mathematics and applications. However, not all functions are continuous. If a function is not continuous at a point in its domain, one says that it has a _____ there. The set of all points of _____ of a function may be a discrete set, a dense set, or even the entire domain of the function.
    a. Discontinuity0
    c. Undefined
    b. Thing
    d. Undefined

51. In common philosophical language, a proposition or _____, is the content of an assertion, that is, it is true-or-false and defined by the meaning of a particular piece of language.
    a. Concept
    c. Undefined
    b. Statement0
    d. Undefined

52. _____, in economics and political economy, are the distributions or payments awarded to the various suppliers of the factors of production.
    a. Thing
    c. Undefined
    b. Returns0
    d. Undefined

53. According to _____ relationship, in a production system with fixed and variable inputs, beyond some point, each additional unit of variable input yields less and less additional output.
    a. Thing
    c. Undefined
    b. Diminishing returns0
    d. Undefined

54. _____ or investing is a term with several closely-related meanings in business management, finance and economics, related to saving or deferring consumption.
    a. Investment0
    c. Undefined
    b. Thing
    d. Undefined

55. The _____ of a ring R is defined to be the smallest positive integer n such that $n\, a = 0$, for all a in R.
    a. Thing
    c. Undefined
    b. Characteristic0
    d. Undefined

56. In mathematics, the _____ f is the collection of all ordered pairs. In particular, graph means the graphical representation of this collection, in the form of a curve or surface, together with axes, etc. Graphing on a Cartesian plane is sometimes referred to as curve sketching.
    a. Graph of a function0
    c. Undefined
    b. Thing
    d. Undefined

57. In mathematics, an _____, mean, or central tendency of a data set refers to a measure of the "middle" or "expected" value of the data set.

a. Concept
b. Average0
c. Undefined
d. Undefined

58. In mathematics, in the field of group theory, a _____ of a group is a quasisimple subnormal subgroup.
   a. Concept
   b. Component0
   c. Undefined
   d. Undefined

59. A frame of _____ is a particular perspective from which the universe is observed.
   a. Reference0
   b. Thing
   c. Undefined
   d. Undefined

60. _____ is a synonym for information.
   a. Data0
   b. Thing
   c. Undefined
   d. Undefined

61. In business, particularly accounting, a _____ is the time intervals that the accounts, statement, payments, or other calculations cover.
   a. Thing
   b. Period0
   c. Undefined
   d. Undefined

62. A _____, scatter diagram or scatter graph is a chart that uses Cartesian coordinates to display values for two variables.
   a. Thing
   b. Scatter plot0
   c. Undefined
   d. Undefined

63. In computer science, an _____ is the problem of finding the best solution from all feasible solutions.
   a. Optimization problem0
   b. Thing
   c. Undefined
   d. Undefined

64. The _____ of a solid object is the three-dimensional concept of how much space it occupies, often quantified numerically.
   a. Thing
   b. Volume0
   c. Undefined
   d. Undefined

65. In plane geometry, a _____ is a polygon with four equal sides, four right angles, and parallel opposite sides. In algebra, the _____ of a number is that number multiplied by itself.
   a. Thing
   b. Square0
   c. Undefined
   d. Undefined

66. A _____ is a symbolic representation denoting a quantity or expression. It often represents an "unknown" quantity that has the potential to change.
   a. Thing
   b. Variable0
   c. Undefined
   d. Undefined

67. A _____ is a simplified and structured visual representation of concepts, ideas, constructions, relations, statistical data, anatomy etc used in all aspects of human activities to visualize and clarify the topic.

Chapter 4. Applications of the Derivative

    a. Diagram0
    b. Thing
    c. Undefined
    d. Undefined

68. A _____ is the result of the addition of a set of numbers. The numbers may be natural numbers, complex numbers, matrices, or still more complicated objects. An infinite _____ is a subtle procedure known as a series.
    a. Sum0
    b. Thing
    c. Undefined
    d. Undefined

69. In finance, a _____ is collateral that the holder of a position in securities, options, or futures contracts has to deposit to cover the credit risk of his counterparty.
    a. Thing
    b. Margin0
    c. Undefined
    d. Undefined

70. In geometry, a _____ is defined as a quadrilateral where all four of its angles are right angles.
    a. Thing
    b. Rectangle0
    c. Undefined
    d. Undefined

71. In mathematics, _____ geometry was the traditional name for the geometry of three-dimensional Euclidean space — for practical purposes the kind of space we live in.
    a. Solid0
    b. Thing
    c. Undefined
    d. Undefined

72. In mathematics, a _____ is a quadric surface, with the following equation in Cartesian coordinates: $(x/_a)^2 + (y/_b)^2 = 1$.
    a. Thing
    b. Cylinder0
    c. Undefined
    d. Undefined

73. In geometry, _____ angles are angles that have a common ray coming out of the vertex going between two other rays.
    a. Concept
    b. Adjacent0
    c. Undefined
    d. Undefined

74. A _____ is a large group of animals. The term is usually applied to mammals, particularly ungulates. Other terms are used for similar phenomena in other types of animal.
    a. Herd0
    b. Thing
    c. Undefined
    d. Undefined

75. In topology and related areas of mathematics a _____ or Moore-Smith sequence is a generalization of a sequence, intended to unify the various notions of limit and generalize them to arbitrary topological spaces.
    a. Net0
    b. Thing
    c. Undefined
    d. Undefined

76. A _____ is one of the basic shapes of geometry: a polygon with three vertices and three sides which are straight line segments.

Chapter 4. Applications of the Derivative

    a. Triangle0
    c. Undefined
    b. Thing
    d. Undefined

77. A _____ consists of one quarter of the coordinate plane.
    a. Quadrant0
    b. Thing
    c. Undefined
    d. Undefined

78. In geometry, a _____ is a special kind of point, usually a corner of a polygon, polyhedron, or higher dimensional polytope. In the geometry of curves a _____ is a point of where the first derivative of curvature is zero. In graph theory, a _____ is the fundamental unit out of which graphs are formed
    a. Vertex0
    b. Thing
    c. Undefined
    d. Undefined

79. _____ is a kind of property which exists as magnitude or multitude. It is among the basic classes of things along with quality, substance, change, and relation.
    a. Thing
    b. Amount0
    c. Undefined
    d. Undefined

80. Compass and straightedge or ruler-and-compass _____ is the _____ of lengths or angles using only an idealized ruler and compass.
    a. Thing
    b. Construction0
    c. Undefined
    d. Undefined

81. In mathematics, a _____ is the set of all points in three-dimensional space (R^3) which are at distance r from a fixed point of that space, where r is a positive real number called the radius of the _____. The fixed point is called the center or centre, and is not part of the _____ itself.
    a. Thing
    b. Sphere0
    c. Undefined
    d. Undefined

82. In Euclidean geometry, a _____ is the set of all points in a plane at a fixed distance, called the radius, from a given point, the center.
    a. Circle0
    b. Thing
    c. Undefined
    d. Undefined

83. _____ is the distance around a given two-dimensional object. As a general rule, the _____ of a polygon can always be calculated by adding all the length of the sides together. So, the formula for triangles is P = a + b + c, where a, b and c stand for each side of it. For quadrilaterals the equation is P = a + b + c + d. For equilateral polygons, P = na, where n is the number of sides and a is the side length.
    a. Perimeter0
    b. Thing
    c. Undefined
    d. Undefined

84. In geometry, an _____ polygon is a polygon which has all sides of the same length.
    a. Equilateral0
    b. Thing
    c. Undefined
    d. Undefined

85. An _____ is a triangle in which all sides are of equal length.

Chapter 4. Applications of the Derivative

    a. Equilateral triangle0
    b. Thing
    c. Undefined
    d. Undefined

86. A _____ is a unit of length, usually used to measure distance, in a number of different systems, including Imperial units, United States customary units and Norwegian/Swedish mil. Its size can vary from system to system, but in each is between 1 and 10 kilometers. In contemporary English contexts _____ refers to either:
    a. Thing
    b. Mile0
    c. Undefined
    d. Undefined

87. In geometry, a _____ is the intersection of a body in 2-dimensional space with a line, or of a body in 3-dimensional space with a plane
    a. Thing
    b. Cross section0
    c. Undefined
    d. Undefined

88. In mathematics, _____ refers to the rewriting of an expression into a simpler form.
    a. Reduction0
    b. Thing
    c. Undefined
    d. Undefined

89. In economics, supply and _____ describe market relations between prospective sellers and buyers of a good.
    a. Thing
    b. Demand0
    c. Undefined
    d. Undefined

90. _____ is the change in total cost that arises when the quantity produced changes by one unit.
    a. Marginal cost0
    b. Thing
    c. Undefined
    d. Undefined

91. _____ is the extra revenue that an additional unit of product will bring a firm. It can also be described as the change in total revenue/change in number of units sold.
    a. Marginal revenue0
    b. Thing
    c. Undefined
    d. Undefined

92. A _____ is an individual or household that purchases and uses goods and services generated within the economy.
    a. Thing
    b. Consumer0
    c. Undefined
    d. Undefined

93. In economics and business studies, the _____ is an elasticity that measures the nature and degree of the relationship between changes in quantity demanded of a good and changes in its price.
    a. Thing
    b. Elasticity of demand0
    c. Undefined
    d. Undefined

94. A _____ is a function that assigns a number to subsets of a given set.
    a. Measure0
    b. Thing
    c. Undefined
    d. Undefined

95. _____ is a way of expressing a number as a fraction of 100 per cent meaning "per hundred".

a. Thing
c. Undefined
b. Percent0
d. Undefined

96. A _____ is a numeral used to indicate a count. The most common use of the word today is to name the part of a fraction that tells the number or count of equal parts.
   a. Numerator0
   b. Thing
   c. Undefined
   d. Undefined

97. A _____ is the part of a fraction that tells how many equal parts make up a whole, and which is used in the name of the fraction: "halves", "thirds", "fourths" or "quarters", "fifths" and so on.
   a. Denominator0
   b. Concept
   c. Undefined
   d. Undefined

98. Fixed costs are expenses whose total does not change in proportion to the activity of a business.Unit fixed costs decline with volume following a retangular hyperbola as the volume of production.Variable costs by contrast change in relation to the activity of a business such as sales or production volume.Along with variable costs,fixed costs make up one of the two components of total cost. In the most simple production function total cost is equal to fixed costs plus variable costs.In accounting terminology, fixed costs will broadly include all costs which are not included in cost of goods sold, and variable costs are those captured in costs of goods sold. The implicit assumption required to make the equivalence between the accounting and economics terminology is that the accounting period is equal to the period in which fixed costs do not vary in relation to production. In practice, this equivalence does not always hold and depending on the period under consideration by management, some overhead expenses can be adjusted by management, and the specific allocation of each expense to each category will be decided under cost accounting.In business planning and management accounting, usage of the terms fixed costs, variable costs and others will often differ from usage in economics, and may depend on the intended use. For example, costs may be segregated into per unit costs fixed costs per period, and variable costs as a proportion of revenue. Capital expenditures will usually be allocated separately, and depending on the purpose, a portion may be regularly allocated to expenses as depreciation and amortization and seen as a _____ per period, or the entire amount may be considered upfront fixed costs.
   a. Fixed cost0
   b. Thing
   c. Undefined
   d. Undefined

99. _____ is the fee paid on borrowed money.
   a. Interest0
   b. Thing
   c. Undefined
   d. Undefined

100. An _____ is the fee paid on borrow money.
   a. Concept
   b. Interest rate0
   c. Undefined
   d. Undefined

101. _____ has many meanings, most of which simply .
   a. Power0
   b. Thing
   c. Undefined
   d. Undefined

102. _____ is a unit of speed, expressing the number of international miles covered per hour.

Chapter 4. Applications of the Derivative

a. Miles per hour0
b. Thing
c. Undefined
d. Undefined

103. A _____ is a compensation which workers receive in exchange for their labor.
   a. Thing
   b. Wage0
   c. Undefined
   d. Undefined

104. _____ is the application of tools and a processing medium to the transformation of raw materials into finished goods for sale.
   a. Manufacturing0
   b. Thing
   c. Undefined
   d. Undefined

105. A _____ is an abstract model that uses mathematical language to describe the behavior of a system. Eykhoff defined a _____ as 'a representation of the essential aspects of an existing system which presents knowledge of that system in usable form'.
   a. Thing
   b. Mathematical model0
   c. Undefined
   d. Undefined

106. _____ is a straight line or curve A to which another curve B the one being studied approaches closer and closer as one moves along it.
   a. Thing
   b. Vertical asymptote0
   c. Undefined
   d. Undefined

107. An _____ is a straight line or curve A to which another curve B approaches closer and closer as one moves along it. As one moves along B, the space between it and the _____ A becomes smaller and smaller, and can in fact be made as small as one could wish by going far enough along. A curve may or may not touch or cross its _____. In fact, the curve may intersect the _____ an infinite number of times.
   a. Asymptote0
   b. Thing
   c. Undefined
   d. Undefined

108. _____ is the state of being greater than any finite real or natural number, however large.
   a. Infinite0
   b. Thing
   c. Undefined
   d. Undefined

109. _____ is the state of being greater than any finite number, however large.
   a. Thing
   b. Infinity0
   c. Undefined
   d. Undefined

110. In astronomy, geography, geometry and related sciences and contexts, a plane is said to be _____ at a given point if it is locally perpendicular to the gradient of the gravity field, i.e., with the direction of the gravitational force at that point.
   a. Thing
   b. Horizontal0
   c. Undefined
   d. Undefined

111. In mathematics, a _____ number is a number which can be expressed as a ratio of two integers. Non-integer _____ numbers (commonly called fractions) are usually written as the vulgar fraction a / b, where b is not zero.

Chapter 4. Applications of the Derivative

a. Thing
b. Rational0
c. Undefined
d. Undefined

112. In mathematics, a _____ is any function which can be written as the ratio of two polynomial functions.
a. Thing
b. Rational function0
c. Undefined
d. Undefined

113. In mathematics, a _____ is an expression that is constructed from one or more variables and constants, using only the operations of addition, subtraction, multiplication, and constant positive whole number exponents. is a _____. Note in particular that division by an expression containing a variable is not in general allowed in polynomials. [1]
a. Polynomial0
b. Thing
c. Undefined
d. Undefined

114. In mathematics, a _____ may be described informally as a number that can be given by an infinite decimal representation.
a. Real number0
b. Thing
c. Undefined
d. Undefined

115. In mathematics, factorization (British English: factorisation) or factoring is the decomposition of an object (for example, a number, a polynomial, or a matrix) into a product of other objects, or _____, which when multiplied together give the original.
a. Factors0
b. Thing
c. Undefined
d. Undefined

116. In mathematics, a _____ is a constant multiplicative factor of a certain object. The object can be such things as a variable, a vector, a function, etc. For example, the _____ of $9x^2$ is 9.
a. Coefficient0
b. Thing
c. Undefined
d. Undefined

117. In mathematics, an inequality is a statement about the relative size or order of two objects. For example 14 > 10, or 14 is _____ 10.
a. Thing
b. Greater than0
c. Undefined
d. Undefined

118. Initial objects are also called _____, and terminal objects are also called final.
a. Thing
b. Coterminal0
c. Undefined
d. Undefined

119. Any point where a graph makes contact with an coordinate axis is called an _____ of the graph
a. Thing
b. Intercept0
c. Undefined
d. Undefined

120. The _____ refers to a relationship between the duration of learning or experience and the resulting progress
a. Thing
b. Learning curve0
c. Undefined
d. Undefined

Chapter 4. Applications of the Derivative

121. _____ refers to all non-domesticated plants, animals, and other organisms.
    a. Thing
    b. Wildlife0
    c. Undefined
    d. Undefined

122. The payment of _____ as remuneration for services rendered or products sold is a common way to reward sales people.
    a. Commission0
    b. Thing
    c. Undefined
    d. Undefined

123. In sociology and biology a _____ is the collection of people or organisms of a particular species living in a given geographic area or space, usually measured by a census.
    a. Thing
    b. Population0
    c. Undefined
    d. Undefined

124. _____ is the study of geometry using the principles of algebra. _____ can be explained more simply: it is concerned with defining geometrical shapes in a numerical way and extracting numerical information from that representation.
    a. Analytic geometry0
    b. Thing
    c. Undefined
    d. Undefined

125. _____ was a highly influential French philosopher, mathematician, scientist, and writer. Dubbed the "Founder of Modern Philosophy", and the "Father of Modern Mathematics". His theories provided the basis for the calculus of Newton and Leibniz, by applying infinitesimal calculus to the tangent line problem, thus permitting the evolution of that branch of modern mathematics
    a. Descartes0
    b. Person
    c. Undefined
    d. Undefined

126. In mathematics, the _____ of a function is the set of all "output" values produced by that function. Given a function $f : A \to B$, the _____ of f, is defined to be the set $\{x \in B : x = f(a)$ for some $a \in A\}$.
    a. Thing
    b. Range0
    c. Undefined
    d. Undefined

127. _____ is a branch of mathematics concerning the study of structure, relation and quantity.
    a. Concept
    b. Algebra0
    c. Undefined
    d. Undefined

128. In mathematics, _____ is the decomposition of an object into a product of other objects, or factors, which when multiplied together give the original.
    a. Factoring0
    b. Thing
    c. Undefined
    d. Undefined

129. Graphing on a Cartesian plane is sometimes referred to as _____.
    a. Curve sketching0
    b. Thing
    c. Undefined
    d. Undefined

130. A _____ is a polynomial function of the form $f(x) = ax^2 + bx + c$, where a, b, c are real numbers and a , 0.

Chapter 4. Applications of the Derivative

    a. Event
    c. Undefined
    b. Quadratic function0
    d. Undefined

131. _____ is a function of the form
    a. Cubic function0
    c. Undefined
    b. Thing
    d. Undefined

132. In mathematics, the _____ is a conic section generated by the intersection of a right circular conical surface and a plane parallel to a generating straight line of that surface. It can also be defined as locus of points in a plane which are equidistant from a given point.
    a. Thing
    c. Undefined
    b. Parabola0
    d. Undefined

133. _____ is a function whose values do not vary and thus are constant.
    a. Constant function0
    c. Undefined
    b. Thing
    d. Undefined

134. _____ is often used to describe the measurement of the steepness, incline, gradient, or grade of a straight line. The _____ is defined as the ratio of the "rise" divided by the "run" between two points on a line, or in other words, the ratio of the altitude change to the horizontal distance between any two points on the line.
    a. Slope0
    c. Undefined
    b. Thing
    d. Undefined

135. In Euclidean geometry, a uniform _____ is a linear transformation that enlargers or diminishes objects, and whose _____ factor is the same in all directions. This is also called homothethy.
    a. Scale0
    c. Undefined
    b. Thing
    d. Undefined

136. U.S. liquid _____ is legally defined as 231 cubic inches, and is equal to 3.785411784 litres or abotu 0.13368 cubic feet. This is the most common definition of a _____. The U.S. fluid ounce is defined as 1/128 of a U.S. _____.
    a. Gallon0
    c. Undefined
    b. Thing
    d. Undefined

137. In combinatorial mathematics, a _____ is an un-ordered collection of unique elements.
    a. Combination0
    c. Undefined
    b. Concept
    d. Undefined

138. In geometry, the _____ of an object is a point in some sense in the middle of the object.
    a. Thing
    c. Undefined
    b. Center0
    d. Undefined

139. A _____ is traditionally an infinitesimally small change in a variable.
    a. Differential0
    c. Undefined
    b. Thing
    d. Undefined

Chapter 4. Applications of the Derivative

140. In mathematics, a _____ is the end result of a division problem. It can also be expressed as the number of times the divisor divides into the dividend.
 a. Quotient0
 b. Thing
 c. Undefined
 d. Undefined

141. _____ is the use of marginal concepts within economics. Marginal concepts include marginal cost, marginal productivity and marginal utility, the law of diminishing rates of substitution, and the law of diminishing marginal utility.
 a. Marginal analysis0
 b. Thing
 c. Undefined
 d. Undefined

142. In mathematics, _____ are the intuitive idea of a geometrical one-dimensional and continuous object.
 a. Curves0
 b. Thing
 c. Undefined
 d. Undefined

143. _____ is the calculated approximation of a result which is usable even if input data may be incomplete, uncertain, or noisy.
 a. Estimation0
 b. Concept
 c. Undefined
 d. Undefined

144. In navigation, a _____ is the clockwise angle between a reference direction and the direction to an object.
 a. Thing
 b. Bearing0
 c. Undefined
 d. Undefined

145. In the mathematical field of numerical analysis, the _____ in some data is the discrepancy between an exact value and some approximation to it.
 a. Thing
 b. Approximation Error0
 c. Undefined
 d. Undefined

146. The word _____ comes from the Latin word linearis, which means created by lines.
 a. Linear0
 b. Thing
 c. Undefined
 d. Undefined

147. A _____ is a first degree polynomial mathematical function of the form: f(x) = mx + b where m and b are real constants and x is a real variable.
 a. Linear function0
 b. Thing
 c. Undefined
 d. Undefined

148. In mathematics, a _____ of a number x is a number r such that r^2 = x, or in words, a number r whose square (the result of multiplying the number by itself) is x.
 a. Thing
 b. Square root0
 c. Undefined
 d. Undefined

149. In mathematics, a _____ of a complex-valued function f is a member x of the domain of f such that f(x) vanishes at x, that is, x : f (x) = 0.

Chapter 4. Applications of the Derivative

   a. Thing
   c. Undefined
   b. Root0
   d. Undefined

150. A _____ is a negotiable instrument instructing a financial institution to pay a specific amount of a specific currency from a specific demand account held in the maker/depositor's name with that institution. Both the maker and payee may be natural persons or legal entities.
   a. Check0
   c. Undefined
   b. Thing
   d. Undefined

151. _____ refers to the reduction of the body of a formerly living organism into simpler forms of matter.
   a. Decomposing0
   c. Undefined
   b. Thing
   d. Undefined

152. _____ is a list of goods and materials, or those goods and materials themselves, held available in stock by a business
   a. Thing
   c. Undefined
   b. Inventory0
   d. Undefined

153. _____ is the level of functional and/or metabolic efficiency of an organism at both the micro level.
   a. Health0
   c. Undefined
   b. Thing
   d. Undefined

154. In geometry, a _____ (Greek words diairo = divide and metro = measure) of a circle is any straight line segment that passes through the centre and whose endpoints are on the circular boundary, or, in more modern usage, the length of such a line segment. When using the word in the more modern sense, one speaks of the _____ rather than a _____, because all diameters of a circle have the same length. This length is twice the radius. The _____ of a circle is also the longest chord that the circle has.
   a. Diameter0
   c. Undefined
   b. Thing
   d. Undefined

155. _____ is the value of a coin or paper money, as printed on the coin or bill itself by the minting authority.
   a. Concept
   c. Undefined
   b. Face value0
   d. Undefined

156. _____ finance, in finance, a debt security, issued by Issuer
   a. Bond0
   c. Undefined
   b. Thing
   d. Undefined

Chapter 5. Exponential and Logarithmic Functions

1. A _____ is a symbolic representation denoting a quantity or expression. It often represents an "unknown" quantity that has the potential to change.
   - a. Variable0
   - b. Thing
   - c. Undefined
   - d. Undefined

2. In mathematics, _____ growth occurs when the growth rate of a function is always proportional to the function's current size.
   - a. Exponential0
   - b. Thing
   - c. Undefined
   - d. Undefined

3. _____ is one of the most important functions in mathematics. A function commonly used to study growth and decay
   - a. Exponential function0
   - b. Thing
   - c. Undefined
   - d. Undefined

4. _____ is informally a function which satisfies a polynomial equation whose coefficients are themselves polynomials.
   - a. Thing
   - b. Algebraic function0
   - c. Undefined
   - d. Undefined

5. _____ has many meanings, most of which simply .
   - a. Thing
   - b. Power0
   - c. Undefined
   - d. Undefined

6. In mathematics and the mathematical sciences, a _____ is a fixed, but possibly unspecified, value. This is in contrast to a variable, which is not fixed.
   - a. Thing
   - b. Constant0
   - c. Undefined
   - d. Undefined

7. The mathematical concept of a _____ expresses the intuitive idea of deterministic dependence between two quantities, one of which is viewed as primary and the other as secondary. A _____ then is a way to associate a unique output for each input of a specified type, for example, a real number or an element of a given set.
   - a. Thing
   - b. Function0
   - c. Undefined
   - d. Undefined

8. _____ is a function whose values do not vary and thus are constant.
   - a. Thing
   - b. Constant function0
   - c. Undefined
   - d. Undefined

9. _____ is a mathematical operation, written a^n, involving two numbers, the base a and the exponent n.
   - a. Exponentiating0
   - b. Thing
   - c. Undefined
   - d. Undefined

10. _____ is a mathematical operation, written a^n, involving two numbers, the base a and the exponent n.
    - a. Thing
    - b. Exponentiation0
    - c. Undefined
    - d. Undefined

Chapter 5. Exponential and Logarithmic Functions

11. An _____ is a combination of numbers, operators, grouping symbols and/or free variables and bound variables arranged in a meaningful way which can be evaluated..
    a. Thing
    b. Expression0
    c. Undefined
    d. Undefined

12. In mathematics, a _____ number is a number which can be expressed as a ratio of two integers. Non-integer _____ numbers (commonly called fractions) are usually written as the vulgar fraction a / b, where b is not zero.
    a. Thing
    b. Rational0
    c. Undefined
    d. Undefined

13. A _____ is a quantity that denotes the proportional amount or magnitude of one quantity relative to another.
    a. Ratio0
    b. Thing
    c. Undefined
    d. Undefined

14. In business, particularly accounting, a _____ is the time intervals that the accounts, statement, payments, or other calculations cover.
    a. Thing
    b. Period0
    c. Undefined
    d. Undefined

15. _____ are the basic objects of study in graph theory. Informally speaking, a graph is a set of objects called points, nodes, or vertices connected by links called lines or edges.
    a. Graphs0
    b. Thing
    c. Undefined
    d. Undefined

16. An _____ is a straight line or curve A to which another curve B approaches closer and closer as one moves along it. As one moves along B, the space between it and the _____ A becomes smaller and smaller, and can in fact be made as small as one could wish by going far enough along. A curve may or may not touch or cross its _____. In fact, the curve may intersect the _____ an infinite number of times.
    a. Asymptote0
    b. Thing
    c. Undefined
    d. Undefined

17. In astronomy, geography, geometry and related sciences and contexts, a plane is said to be _____ at a given point if it is locally perpendicular to the gradient of the gravity field, i.e., with the direction of the gravitational force at that point.
    a. Horizontal0
    b. Thing
    c. Undefined
    d. Undefined

18. _____ is the process of reducing the number of significant digits in a number.
    a. Rounding0
    b. Concept
    c. Undefined
    d. Undefined

19. _____ is a term used in accounting, economics and finance with reference to the fact that assets with finite lives lose value over time.
    a. Thing
    b. Depreciation0
    c. Undefined
    d. Undefined

20. Initial objects are also called _____, and terminal objects are also called final.

a. Coterminal0
b. Thing
c. Undefined
d. Undefined

21. An _____ or member of a set is an object that when collected together make up the set.
   a. Element0
   b. Thing
   c. Undefined
   d. Undefined

22. _____ is the process in which an unstable atomic nucleus loses energy by emitting radiation in the form of particles or electromagnetic waves.
   a. Thing
   b. Radioactive decay0
   c. Undefined
   d. Undefined

23. _____ is the property of a physical object that quantifies the amount of matter and energy it is equivalent to.
   a. Mass0
   b. Thing
   c. Undefined
   d. Undefined

24. In linear algebra, the _____ of an n-by-n square matrix A is defined to be the sum of the elements on the main diagonal of A,
   a. Thing
   b. Trace0
   c. Undefined
   d. Undefined

25. In geographic information systems, a _____ comprises an entity with a geographic location, typically determined by points, arcs, or polygons. Carriageways and cadastres exemplify _____ data.
   a. Feature0
   b. Thing
   c. Undefined
   d. Undefined

26. _____ is a kind of property which exists as magnitude or multitude. It is among the basic classes of things along with quality, substance, change, and relation.
   a. Amount0
   b. Thing
   c. Undefined
   d. Undefined

27. _____ is a mathematical subject that includes the study of limits, derivatives, integrals, and power series and constitutes a major part of modern university curriculum.
   a. Calculus0
   b. Thing
   c. Undefined
   d. Undcfined

28. In mathematics, a _____ is a countable collection of open covers of a topological space that satisfies certain separation axioms.
   a. Development0
   b. Thing
   c. Undefined
   d. Undefined

29. In mathematics, an _____ number is any real number that is not a rational number- that is, it is a number which cannot be expressed as a fraction m/n, where m and n are integers.
   a. Irrational0
   b. Thing
   c. Undefined
   d. Undefined

Chapter 5. Exponential and Logarithmic Functions

30. In mathematics, an _____ is any real number that is not a rational number ¡ª that is, it is a number which cannot be expressed as m/n, where m and n are integers.
    a. Irrational number0
    b. Thing
    c. Undefined
    d. Undefined

31. In sociology and biology a _____ is the collection of people or organisms of a particular species living in a given geographic area or space, usually measured by a census.
    a. Population0
    b. Thing
    c. Undefined
    d. Undefined

32. _____ is change in population over time, and can be quantified as the change in the number of individuals in a population per unit time.
    a. Population growth0
    b. Thing
    c. Undefined
    d. Undefined

33. _____ is the state of being greater than any finite number, however large.
    a. Thing
    b. Infinity0
    c. Undefined
    d. Undefined

34. _____ is the fee paid on borrowed money.
    a. Interest0
    b. Thing
    c. Undefined
    d. Undefined

35. A _____ is a special kind of ratio, indicating a relationship between two measurements with different units, such as miles to gallons or cents to pounds.
    a. Thing
    b. Rate0
    c. Undefined
    d. Undefined

36. In mathematics, an _____, mean, or central tendency of a data set refers to a measure of the "middle" or "expected" value of the data set.
    a. Concept
    b. Average0
    c. Undefined
    d. Undefined

37. A _____ are accounts maintained by commercial banks, savings and loan associations, credit unions, and mutual savings banks that pay interest but can not be used directly as money by, for example, writing a cheque.
    a. Savings account0
    b. Thing
    c. Undefined
    d. Undefined

38. An _____ is the fee paid on borrow money.
    a. Concept
    b. Interest rate0
    c. Undefined
    d. Undefined

39. In banking and accountancy, the outstanding _____ is the amount of money owned, or due, that remains in a deposit account or a loan account at a given date, after all past remittances, payments and withdrawal have been accounted for.

Chapter 5. Exponential and Logarithmic Functions

a. Balance0
b. Thing
c. Undefined
d. Undefined

40. In common philosophical language, a proposition or _____, is the content of an assertion, that is, it is true-or-false and defined by the meaning of a particular piece of language.
   a. Concept
   b. Statement0
   c. Undefined
   d. Undefined

41. In statistics the _____ of an event i is the number n_i of times the event occurred in the experiment or the study. These frequencies are often graphically represented in histograms.
   a. Concept
   b. Frequency0
   c. Undefined
   d. Undefined

42. _____ generally derives from name. A _____ quantity e.g., length, diameter, volume, voltage, value is generally the quantity according to which some item has been named or is generally referred to.
   a. Nominal0
   b. Thing
   c. Undefined
   d. Undefined

43. _____ is an expression of the effective interest rate that will be paid on a loan, taking into account one-time fees and standardizing the way the rate is expressed.
   a. Thing
   b. Annual percentage rate0
   c. Undefined
   d. Undefined

44. _____ of a single or multiple future payments is the nominal amounts of money to change hands at some future date, discounted to account for the time value of money, and other factors such as investment risk.
   a. Thing
   b. Present value0
   c. Undefined
   d. Undefined

45. _____ interest refers to the fact that whenever interest is calculated, it is based not only on the original principal, but also on any unpaid interest that has been added to the principal.
   a. Thing
   b. Compound0
   c. Undefined
   d. Undefined

46. _____ refers to the fact that whenever interest is calculated, it is based not only on the original principal, but also on any unpaid interest that has been added to the principal. The more frequently interest is compounded, the faster the balance grows.
   a. Concept
   b. Compound interest0
   c. Undefined
   d. Undefined

47. _____ or investing is a term with several closely-related meanings in business management, finance and economics, related to saving or deferring consumption.
   a. Investment0
   b. Thing
   c. Undefined
   d. Undefined

48. A _____ or CD is a time deposit, a financial product commonly offered to consumers by banks, thrift institutions, and credit unions.

Chapter 5. Exponential and Logarithmic Functions

a. Thing
c. Undefined
b. Certificate of deposit0
d. Undefined

49. _____ measures the nominal future sum of money that a given sum of money is "worth" at a specified time in the future assuming a certain interest rate; this value does not include corrections for inflation or other factors that affect the true value of money in the future.
a. Thing
c. Undefined
b. Future value0
d. Undefined

50. In economics, supply and _____ describe market relations between prospective sellers and buyers of a good.
a. Thing
c. Undefined
b. Demand0
d. Undefined

51. _____ is the chance that something is likely to happen or be the case.
a. Thing
c. Undefined
b. Probability0
d. Undefined

52. The _____ of measurement are a globally standardized and modernized form of the metric system.
a. Thing
c. Undefined
b. Units0
d. Undefined

53. In a mathematical proof or a syllogism, a _____ is a statement that is the logical consequence of preceding statements.
a. Conclusion0
c. Undefined
b. Concept
d. Undefined

54. _____ are a measure of time.
a. Thing
c. Undefined
b. Minutes0
d. Undefined

55. _____ is a special mathematical relationship between two quantities. Two quantities are called proportional if they vary in such a way that one of the quantities is a constant multiple of the other, or equivalently if they have a constant ratio.
a. Thing
c. Undefined
b. Proportionality0
d. Undefined

56. A _____ is an individual or household that purchases and uses goods and services generated within the economy.
a. Thing
c. Undefined
b. Consumer0
d. Undefined

57. _____ consists of the knowledge of various products to protect the public from fraudulent or unforseeable circumstances.
a. Consumer awareness0
c. Undefined
b. Thing
d. Undefined

Chapter 5. Exponential and Logarithmic Functions

58. A _____ is a unit of length, usually used to measure distance, in a number of different systems, including Imperial units, United States customary units and Norwegian/Swedish mil. Its size can vary from system to system, but in each is between 1 and 10 kilometers. In contemporary English contexts _____ refers to either:
   a. Thing
   b. Mile0
   c. Undefined
   d. Undefined

59. _____ is a unit of speed, expressing the number of international miles covered per hour.
   a. Thing
   b. Miles per hour0
   c. Undefined
   d. Undefined

60. U.S. liquid _____ is legally defined as 231 cubic inches, and is equal to 3.785411784 litres or abotu 0.13368 cubic feet. This is the most common definition of a _____. The U.S. fluid ounce is defined as 1/128 of a U.S. _____.
   a. Gallon0
   b. Thing
   c. Undefined
   d. Undefined

61. In mathematics, an inequality is a statement about the relative size or order of two objects. For example 14 > 10, or 14 is _____ 10.
   a. Thing
   b. Greater than0
   c. Undefined
   d. Undefined

62. The _____ is a measurement of how a function changes when the values of its inputs change.
   a. Derivative0
   b. Thing
   c. Undefined
   d. Undefined

63. _____ is a function that represents a probability distribution in terms of integrals.
   a. Thing
   b. Probability density function0
   c. Undefined
   d. Undefined

64. _____ is mass m per unit volume V.
   a. Density0
   b. Thing
   c. Undefined
   d. Undefined

65. A _____ is a numeral used to indicate a count. The most common use of the word today is to name the part of a fraction that tells the number or count of equal parts.
   a. Thing
   b. Numerator0
   c. Undefined
   d. Undefined

66. In calculus, the _____ is a formula for the derivative of the composite of two functions.
   a. Chain rule0
   b. Concept
   c. Undefined
   d. Undefined

67. In trigonometry, the _____ is a function defined as $\tan x = \sin x / \cos x$. The function is so-named because it can be defined as the length of a certain segment of a _____ (in the geometric sense) to the unit circle. In plane geometry, a line is _____ to a curve, at some point, if both line and curve pass through the point with the same direction.

Chapter 5. Exponential and Logarithmic Functions

    a. Tangent0   b. Thing
    c. Undefined   d. Undefined

68. _____ has two distinct but etymologically-related meanings: one in geometry and one in trigonometry.
    a. Tangent line0   b. Thing
    c. Undefined   d. Undefined

69. _____, a field in mathematics, is the study of how functions change when their inputs change. The primary object of study in _____ is the derivative.
    a. Differential calculus0   b. Thing
    c. Undefined   d. Undefined

70. In mathematics, the concept of a _____ tries to capture the intuitive idea of a geometrical one-dimensional and continuous object. A simple example is the circle.
    a. Curve0   b. Thing
    c. Undefined   d. Undefined

71. _____ is the shape of a hanging flexible chain or cable when supported at its ends and acted upon by a uniform gravitational force. The chain is steepest near the points of suspension because this part of the chain has the most weight pulling down on it. Toward the bottom, the slope of the chain decreases because the chain is supporting less weight.
    a. Thing   b. Catenary0
    c. Undefined   d. Undefined

72. The _____ is the lowest point in a certain portion of a graph.
    a. Relative minimum0   b. Thing
    c. Undefined   d. Undefined

73. In elementary algebra, an _____ is a set that contains every real number between two indicated numbers and may contain the two numbers themselves.
    a. Thing   b. Interval0
    c. Undefined   d. Undefined

74. _____ is the middle point of a line segment.
    a. Midpoint0   b. Thing
    c. Undefined   d. Undefined

75. _____ is the extra revenue that an additional unit of product will bring a firm. It can also be described as the change in total revenue/change in number of units sold.
    a. Thing   b. Marginal revenue0
    c. Undefined   d. Undefined

76. _____ is a business term for the amount of money that a company receives from its activities in a given period, mostly from sales of products and/or services to customers
    a. Revenue0   b. Thing
    c. Undefined   d. Undefined

Chapter 5. Exponential and Logarithmic Functions

77. In mathematics, a _____ is the result of multiplying, or an expression that identifies factors to be multiplied.
    a. Thing
    b. Product0
    c. Undefined
    d. Undefined

78. _____ is the eighteenth letter of the Greek alphabet.
    a. Thing
    b. Sigma0
    c. Undefined
    d. Undefined

79. The _____ of a ring R is defined to be the smallest positive integer n such that n a = 0, for all a in R.
    a. Thing
    b. Characteristic0
    c. Undefined
    d. Undefined

80. _____ is a mathematical science pertaining to the collection, analysis, interpretation or explanation, and presentation of data. It is applicable to a wide variety of academic disciplines, from the physical and social sciences to the humanities.
    a. Statistics0
    b. Thing
    c. Undefined
    d. Undefined

81. in mathematics, maxima and minima, known collectively as _____, are the largest value maximum or smallest value minimum, that a function takes in a point either within a given neighborhood or on the function domain in its entirety global extremum.
    a. Thing
    b. Extrema0
    c. Undefined
    d. Undefined

82. _____ is often used to describe the measurement of the steepness, incline, gradient, or grade of a straight line. The _____ is defined as the ratio of the "rise" divided by the "run" between two points on a line, or in other words, the ratio of the altitude change to the horizontal distance between any two points on the line.
    a. Slope0
    b. Thing
    c. Undefined
    d. Undefined

83. The word _____ comes from the Latin word linearis, which means created by lines.
    a. Thing
    b. Linear0
    c. Undefined
    d. Undefined

84. _____ is a way of expressing a number as a fraction of 100 per cent meaning "per hundred".
    a. Percent0
    b. Thing
    c. Undefined
    d. Undefined

85. _____ is the art, science, and practice of studying and managing forests and plantations, and related natural resources.
    a. Forestry0
    b. Thing
    c. Undefined
    d. Undefined

86. _____ of a probability distribution, random variable, or population or multiset of values is a measure of the spread of its values.

Chapter 5. Exponential and Logarithmic Functions

a. Standard deviation0
c. Undefined
b. Thing
d. Undefined

87. _____ is a synonym for information.
a. Data0
c. Undefined
b. Thing
d. Undefined

88. The _____, the average in everyday English, which is also called the arithmetic _____ (and is distinguished from the geometric _____ or harmonic _____). The average is also called the sample _____. The expected value of a random variable, which is also called the population _____.
a. Mean0
c. Undefined
b. Thing
d. Undefined

89. _____ is a measure of difference for interval and ratio variables between the observed value and the mean.
a. Thing
c. Undefined
b. Deviation0
d. Undefined

90. In mathematics, a _____ is a two-dimensional manifold or surface that is perfectly flat.
a. Plane0
c. Undefined
b. Thing
d. Undefined

91. _____ element of an element x with respect to a binary operation * with identity element e is an element y such that x * y = y * x = e. In particular,
a. Thing
c. Undefined
b. Inverse0
d. Undefined

92. _____ is the logarithm to the base e, where e is an irrational constant approximately equal to 2.718281828459.
a. Thing
c. Undefined
b. Natural logarithm0
d. Undefined

93. In mathematics, a _____ of a number x is the exponent y of the power by such that $x = b^y$. The value used for the base b must be neither 0 nor 1, nor a root of 1 in the case of the extension to complex numbers, and is typically 10, e, or 2.
a. Logarithm0
c. Undefined
b. Thing
d. Undefined

94. _____ is a branch of mathematics concerning the study of structure, relation and quantity.
a. Algebra0
c. Undefined
b. Concept
d. Undefined

95. In mathematics, a _____ (also spelled reflexion) is a map that transforms an object into its mirror image.
a. Concept
c. Undefined
b. Reflection0
d. Undefined

96. A _____ is a number that is less than zero.

Chapter 5. Exponential and Logarithmic Functions

a. Negative number0   b. Thing
c. Undefined   d. Undefined

97. In mathematics, a _____ may be described informally as a number that can be given by an infinite decimal representation.
   a. Thing   b. Real number0
   c. Undefined   d. Undefined

98. In mathematics, a _____ of a k-place relation $L \subseteq X_1 \times ... \times X_k$ is one of the sets X_j, $1 \leq j \leq k$. In the special case where k = 2 and $L \subseteq X_1 \times X_2$ is a function $L : X_1 \to X_2$, it is conventional to refer to X_1 as the _____ of the function and to refer to X_2 as the codomain of the function.
   a. Thing   b. Domain0
   c. Undefined   d. Undefined

99. A _____ function is a function for which, intuitively, small changes in the input result in small changes in the output.
   a. Continuous0   b. Event
   c. Undefined   d. Undefined

100. In mathematics, the _____ of a function is the set of all "output" values produced by that function. Given a function $f : A \to B$, the _____ of f, is defined to be the set $\{x \in B : x = f(a)$ for some $a \in A\}$.
   a. Thing   b. Range0
   c. Undefined   d. Undefined

101. Any point where a graph makes contact with an coordinate axis is called an _____ of the graph
   a. Intercept0   b. Thing
   c. Undefined   d. Undefined

102. In mathematics, a _____ is a number in the form of a + bi where a and b are real numbers, and i is the imaginary unit, with the property i 2 = −1. The real number a is called the real part of the _____, and the real number b is the imaginary part.
   a. Thing   b. Complex number0
   c. Undefined   d. Undefined

103. In Euclidean geometry, a _____ is moving every point a constant distance in a specified direction.
   a. Concept   b. Translation0
   c. Undefined   d. Undefined

104. A _____ of a number is the product of that number with any integer.
   a. Thing   b. Multiple0
   c. Undefined   d. Undefined

105. A _____ is the result of the addition of a set of numbers. The numbers may be natural numbers, complex numbers, matrices, or still more complicated objects. An infinite _____ is a subtle procedure known as a series.

Chapter 5. Exponential and Logarithmic Functions

a. Thing
b. Sum0
c. Undefined
d. Undefined

106. The _____ is the period of time required for a quantity to double in size or value.
a. Thing
b. Doubling time0
c. Undefined
d. Undefined

107. In mathematics, two quantities are called _____ if they vary in such a way that one of the quantities is a constant multiple of the other, or equivalently if they have a constant ratio.
a. Thing
b. Proportional0
c. Undefined
d. Undefined

108. In mathematics, a _____ is an n-tuple with n being 3.
a. Thing
b. Triple0
c. Undefined
d. Undefined

109. _____ usually refers to money in the form of liquid currency, such as banknotes or coins.
a. Thing
b. Cash0
c. Undefined
d. Undefined

110. _____ is a radiometric dating method that uses the naturally occurring isotope carbon-14 to determine the age of carbonaceous materials up to about 60,000 years.
a. Radiocarbon dating0
b. Thing
c. Undefined
d. Undefined

111. Equivalence is the condition of being _____ or essentially equal.
a. Thing
b. Equivalent0
c. Undefined
d. Undefined

112. In Euclidean geometry, a uniform _____ is a linear transformation that enlargers or diminishes objects, and whose _____ factor is the same in all directions. This is also called homothety.
a. Thing
b. Scale0
c. Undefined
d. Undefined

113. _____ is the curve along which a small object moves when pulled on a horizontal plane with a piece of thread by a puller, which moves rectilinearly with infinitesimal speed.
a. Tractrix0
b. Thing
c. Undefined
d. Undefined

114. A frame of _____ is a particular perspective from which the universe is observed.
a. Thing
b. Reference0
c. Undefined
d. Undefined

115. The _____ is the process of converting elements in one basis to another when both describe the same elements of the finite field $GF(p^m)$.

Chapter 5. Exponential and Logarithmic Functions

a. Change of base0
b. Thing
c. Undefined
d. Undefined

116. The _____ is the process of converting elements in one basis to another when both describe the same elements of the finite field $GF(p^m)$.
    a. Thing
    b. Change of bases0
    c. Undefined
    d. Undefined

117. _____ is to give an equation $R(x,y) = S(x,y)$ that at least in part has the same graph as $y = f(x)$.
    a. Thing
    b. Implicit differentiation0
    c. Undefined
    d. Undefined

118. In mathematics, a _____ is the end result of a division problem. It can also be expressed as the number of times the divisor divides into the dividend.
    a. Thing
    b. Quotient0
    c. Undefined
    d. Undefined

119. The _____ is a method of finding the derivative of a function that is the quotient of two other functions for which derivatives exist.
    a. Quotient rule0
    b. Thing
    c. Undefined
    d. Undefined

120. Acid _____ ratio measures the ability of a company to use its near cash or quick assets to immediately extinguish its current liabilities.
    a. Thing
    b. Test0
    c. Undefined
    d. Undefined

121. In mathematics, the _____ is the logarithm with base 10.
    a. Thing
    b. Common logarithm0
    c. Undefined
    d. Undefined

122. In mathematics, a _____ is a demonstration that, assuming certain axioms, some statement is necessarily true.
    a. Thing
    b. Proof0
    c. Undefined
    d. Undefined

123. Deductive _____ is the kind of _____ in which the conclusion is necessitated by, or reached from, previously known facts (the premises).
    a. Thing
    b. Reasoning0
    c. Undefined
    d. Undefined

124. The _____, i.e., acoustic intensity is defined as the sound power P_{ac} per unit area A.
    a. Thing
    b. Sound intensity0
    c. Undefined
    d. Undefined

Chapter 5. Exponential and Logarithmic Functions

125. In plane geometry, a _____ is a polygon with four equal sides, four right angles, and parallel opposite sides. In algebra, the _____ of a number is that number multiplied by itself.
    a. Thing
    b. Square0
    c. Undefined
    d. Undefined

126. The _____ relative to a specified or implied reference level.
    a. Decibel0
    b. Thing
    c. Undefined
    d. Undefined

127. _____ is a physical property of a system that underlies the common notions of hot and cold; something that is hotter has the greater _____.
    a. Temperature0
    b. Thing
    c. Undefined
    d. Undefined

128. A _____ is a method of using property as security for the payment of a debt.
    a. Thing
    b. Mortgage0
    c. Undefined
    d. Undefined

129. A _____ is a landform that extends above the surrounding terrain in a limited area. A _____ is generally steeper than a hill, but there is no universally accepted standard definition for the height of a _____ or a hill although a _____ usually has an identifiable summit.
    a. Mountain0
    b. Thing
    c. Undefined
    d. Undefined

130. A _____ is an abstract model that uses mathematical language to describe the behavior of a system. Eykhoff defined a _____ as 'a representation of the essential aspects of an existing system which presents knowledge of that system in usable form'.
    a. Mathematical model0
    b. Thing
    c. Undefined
    d. Undefined

131. In mathematics, _____ occurs when the growth rate of a function is always proportional to the function's current size.
    a. Thing
    b. Exponential growth0
    c. Undefined
    d. Undefined

132. _____ is a decrease that follows an exponential function.
    a. Thing
    b. Exponential decay0
    c. Undefined
    d. Undefined

133. _____ is a subset of a population.
    a. Thing
    b. Sample0
    c. Undefined
    d. Undefined

134. _____ are any documents that aim to streamline particular processes according to a set routine.

Chapter 5. Exponential and Logarithmic Functions

   a. Thing
   b. Guidelines0
   c. Undefined
   d. Undefined

135. In the scientific method, an _____ (Latin: ex-+-periri, "of (or from) trying"), is a set of actions and observations, performed in the context of solving a particular problem or question, in order to support or falsify a hypothesis or research concerning phenomena.
   a. Thing
   b. Experiment0
   c. Undefined
   d. Undefined

136. _____ is essentially exponential growth based on a constant rate of compound interest.
   a. Exponential growth model0
   b. Thing
   c. Undefined
   d. Undefined

137. _____, or Drosophila Melanoaster is a two-winged insect that belongs to the Diptera, the order of the flies. The species is commonly known as the fruit fly, and is one of the most commonly used model organisms in biology, including studies in genetics, physiology and life history evolution.
   a. Fruit flies0
   b. Thing
   c. Undefined
   d. Undefined

138. In regression analysis, _____, also known as ordinary _____ analysis is a method for linear regression that determines the values of unknown quantities in a statistical model by minimizing the sum of the residuals difference between the predicted and observed values squared.
   a. Thing
   b. Least squares0
   c. Undefined
   d. Undefined

139. The _____ refers to a relationship between the duration of learning or experience and the resulting progress
   a. Thing
   b. Learning curve0
   c. Undefined
   d. Undefined

140. The _____ of a mathematical object is its size: a property by which it can be larger or smaller than other objects of the same kind; in technical terms, an ordering of the class of objects to which it belongs.
   a. Magnitude0
   b. Thing
   c. Undefined
   d. Undefined

141. An _____ is the result from the sudden release of stored energy in the Earth's crust that creates seismic waves.
   a. Earthquake0
   b. Thing
   c. Undefined
   d. Undefined

142. In set theory and its applications throughout mathematics, _____ are a collection of sets (or sometimes other mathematical objects) that can be unambiguously defined by a property that all its members share.
   a. Classes0
   b. Thing
   c. Undefined
   d. Undefined

143. The _____ governs the differentiation of products of differentiable functions.

Chapter 5. Exponential and Logarithmic Functions

a. Thing
c. Undefined

b. Product rule0
d. Undefined

144. In calculus, the _____ in differentiation is a method of finding the derivative of a function that is the sum of two other functions for which derivatives exist.
a. Sum Rule0
c. Undefined

b. Thing
d. Undefined

145. _____, from Latin meaning "to make progress", is defined in two different ways. Pure economic _____ is the increase in wealth that an investor has from making an investment, taking into consideration all costs associated with that investment including the opportunity cost of capital.
a. Thing
c. Undefined

b. Profit0
d. Undefined

146. A _____ is a compensation which workers receive in exchange for their labor.
a. Wage0
c. Undefined

b. Thing
d. Undefined

147. In mainstream economics, the word _____ refers to a general rise in prices measured against a standard level of purchasing power.
a. Inflation0
c. Undefined

b. Thing
d. Undefined

148. _____ refers to the reduction of the body of a formerly living organism into simpler forms of matter.
a. Decomposing0
c. Undefined

b. Thing
d. Undefined

149. _____ are waste types containing radioactive chemical elements that do not have a practical purpose.
a. Radioactive waste0
c. Undefined

b. Thing
d. Undefined

150. A _____ is a fee added to a customer's bill.
a. Service charge0
c. Undefined

b. Thing
d. Undefined

Chapter 6. Integration and Its Applications

1. Mathematical _____ is used to represent ideas.
   a. Notation0
   b. Thing
   c. Undefined
   d. Undefined

2. The _____ of a function is an extension of the concept of a sum, and are identified or found through the use of integration.
   a. Thing
   b. Integral0
   c. Undefined
   d. Undefined

3. An _____ of a function f is a function F whose derivative is equal to f, i.e., F' = f.
   a. Thing
   b. Antiderivative0
   c. Undefined
   d. Undefined

4. _____ is a process of combining or accumulating. It may also refer to:
   a. Integration0
   b. Thing
   c. Undefined
   d. Undefined

5. Initial objects are also called _____, and terminal objects are also called final.
   a. Coterminal0
   b. Thing
   c. Undefined
   d. Undefined

6. In mathematics, in the field of differential equations, an initial value problem is a differential equation together with specified value, called the _____, of the unknown function at a given point in the domain of the solution.
   a. Initial condition0
   b. Thing
   c. Undefined
   d. Undefined

7. _____ is a mathematical subject that includes the study of limits, derivatives, integrals, and power series and constitutes a major part of modern university curriculum.
   a. Calculus0
   b. Thing
   c. Undefined
   d. Undefined

8. The _____ is a measurement of how a function changes when the values of its inputs change.
   a. Derivative0
   b. Thing
   c. Undefined
   d. Undefined

9. The mathematical concept of a _____ expresses the intuitive idea of deterministic dependence between two quantities, one of which is viewed as primary and the other as secondary. A _____ then is a way to associate a unique output for each input of a specified type, for example, a real number or an element of a given set.
   a. Function0
   b. Thing
   c. Undefined
   d. Undefined

10. _____ element of an element x with respect to a binary operation * with identity element e is an element y such that x * y = y * x = e. In particular,
    a. Thing
    b. Inverse0
    c. Undefined
    d. Undefined

11. A _____ is 360° or 2∂ radians.

Chapter 6. Integration and Its Applications

a. Thing
b. Turn0
c. Undefined
d. Undefined

12. _____ in calculus is primitive or indefinite integral of a function f is a function F whose derivative is equal to f, i.e., F Œ = f. The process of solving for antiderivatives is _____
    a. Antidifferentiation0
    b. Thing
    c. Undefined
    d. Undefined

13. In mathematics and the mathematical sciences, a _____ is a fixed, but possibly unspecified, value. This is in contrast to a variable, which is not fixed.
    a. Constant0
    b. Thing
    c. Undefined
    d. Undefined

14. In mathematics, a _____ of a k-place relation $L \subseteq X_1 \times \ldots \times X_k$ is one of the sets X_j, $1 \le j \le k$. In the special case where k = 2 and $L \subseteq X_1 \times X_2$ is a function $L : X_1 \rightarrow X_2$, it is conventional to refer to X_1 as the _____ of the function and to refer to X_2 as the codomain of the function.
    a. Thing
    b. Domain0
    c. Undefined
    d. Undefined

15. _____ is a function that extends the concept of an ordinary sum
    a. Thing
    b. Integrand0
    c. Undefined
    d. Undefined

16. In calculus, the indefinite integral of a given function i.e. the set of all antiderivatives of the function is always written with a constant, the _____.
    a. Constant of integration0
    b. Thing
    c. Undefined
    d. Undefined

17. A _____ is traditionally an infinitesimally small change in a variable.
    a. Differential0
    b. Thing
    c. Undefined
    d. Undefined

18. A _____ is a symbolic representation denoting a quantity or expression. It often represents an "unknown" quantity that has the potential to change.
    a. Variable0
    b. Thing
    c. Undefined
    d. Undefined

19. The _____, the average in everyday English, which is also called the arithmetic _____ (and is distinguished from the geometric _____ or harmonic _____). The average is also called the sample _____. The expected value of a random variable, which is also called the population _____.
    a. Thing
    b. Mean0
    c. Undefined
    d. Undefined

20. A _____ is a set of numbers that designate location in a given reference system, such as x,y in a planar _____ system or an x,y,z in a three-dimensional _____ system.

Chapter 6. Integration and Its Applications

    a. Coordinate0   b. Thing
    c. Undefined   d. Undefined

21. In mathematics, a _____ is a two-dimensional manifold or surface that is perfectly flat.
    a. Thing   b. Plane0
    c. Undefined   d. Undefined

22. _____, a field in mathematics, is the study of how functions change when their inputs change. The primary object of study in _____ is the derivative.
    a. Differential calculus0   b. Thing
    c. Undefined   d. Undefined

23. A _____ of a number is the product of that number with any integer.
    a. Thing   b. Multiple0
    c. Undefined   d. Undefined

24. _____ has many meanings, most of which simply .
    a. Power0   b. Thing
    c. Undefined   d. Undefined

25. _____ is a method for differentiating expressions involving exponentiation the power operation.
    a. Thing   b. Power rule0
    c. Undefined   d. Undefined

26. A _____ is a negotiable instrument instructing a financial institution to pay a specific amount of a specific currency from a specific demand account held in the maker/depositor's name with that institution. Both the maker and payee may be natural persons or legal entities.
    a. Check0   b. Thing
    c. Undefined   d. Undefined

27. In mathematics, a _____ is an expression that is constructed from one or more variables and constants, using only the operations of addition, subtraction, multiplication, and constant positive whole number exponents. is a _____. Note in particular that division by an expression containing a variable is not in general allowed in polynomials. [1]
    a. Polynomial0   b. Thing
    c. Undetined   d. Undcfined

28. A _____ is the result of the addition of a set of numbers. The numbers may be natural numbers, complex numbers, matrices, or still more complicated objects. An infinite _____ is a subtle procedure known as a series.
    a. Sum0   b. Thing
    c. Undefined   d. Undefined

29. In calculus, the _____ in differentiation is a method of finding the derivative of a function that is the sum of two other functions for which derivatives exist.
    a. Sum Rule0   b. Thing
    c. Undefined   d. Undefined

Chapter 6. Integration and Its Applications

30. In mathematics, a _____ is the end result of a division problem. It can also be expressed as the number of times the divisor divides into the dividend.
    a. Quotient0
    b. Thing
    c. Undefined
    d. Undefined

31. In mathematics, a _____ number is a number which can be expressed as a ratio of two integers. Non-integer _____ numbers (commonly called fractions) are usually written as the vulgar fraction a / b, where b is not zero.
    a. Thing
    b. Rational0
    c. Undefined
    d. Undefined

32. _____ is a mathematical operation, written a^n, involving two numbers, the base a and the exponent n.
    a. Thing
    b. Exponentiating0
    c. Undefined
    d. Undefined

33. _____ is a mathematical operation, written a^n, involving two numbers, the base a and the exponent n.
    a. Thing
    b. Exponentiation0
    c. Undefined
    d. Undefined

34. _____ of an object is its speed in a particular direction.
    a. Velocity0
    b. Thing
    c. Undefined
    d. Undefined

35. _____ is defined as the rate of change or derivative with respect to time of velocity.
    a. Thing
    b. Acceleration0
    c. Undefined
    d. Undefined

36. A _____ is a special kind of ratio, indicating a relationship between two measurements with different units, such as miles to gallons or cents to pounds.
    a. Thing
    b. Rate0
    c. Undefined
    d. Undefined

37. In mathematics, a _____ is the result of multiplying, or an expression that identifies factors to be multiplied.
    a. Thing
    b. Product0
    c. Undefined
    d. Undefined

38. The _____ of measurement are a globally standardized and modernized form of the metric system.
    a. Thing
    b. Units0
    c. Undefined
    d. Undefined

39. _____ is the change in total cost that arises when the quantity produced changes by one unit.
    a. Thing
    b. Marginal cost0
    c. Undefined
    d. Undefined

40. An _____ is a combination of numbers, operators, grouping symbols and/or free variables and bound variables arranged in a meaningful way which can be evaluated..

Chapter 6. Integration and Its Applications

   a. Thing
   c. Undefined
   b. Expression0
   d. Undefined

41. In mathematics, a matrix can be thought of as each row or _____ being a vector. Hence, a space formed by row vectors or _____ vectors are said to be a row space or a _____ space.
   a. Concept
   c. Undefined
   b. Column0
   d. Undefined

42. A _____ is a mathematical equation for an unknown function of one or several variables which relates the values of the function itself and of its derivatives of various orders.
   a. Differential equation0
   c. Undefined
   b. Thing
   d. Undefined

43. _____ are the basic objects of study in graph theory. Informally speaking, a graph is a set of objects called points, nodes, or vertices connected by links called lines or edges.
   a. Thing
   c. Undefined
   b. Graphs0
   d. Undefined

44. Fixed costs are expenses whose total does not change in proportion to the activity of a business.Unit fixed costs decline with volume following a retangular hyperbola as the volume of production.Variable costs by contrast change in relation to the activity of a business such as sales or production volume.Along with variable costs,fixed costs make up one of the two components of total cost. In the most simple production function total cost is equal to fixed costs plus variable costs.In accounting terminology, fixed costs will broadly include all costs which are not included in cost of goods sold, and variable costs are those captured in costs of goods sold. The implicit assumption required to make the equivalence between the accounting and economics terminology is that the accounting period is equal to the period in which fixed costs do not vary in relation to production. In practice, this equivalence does not always hold and depending on the period under consideration by management, some overhead expenses can be adjusted by management, and the specific allocation of each expense to each category will be decided under cost accounting.In business planning and management accounting, usage of the terms fixed costs, variable costs and others will often differ from usage in economics, and may depend on the intended use. For example, costs may be segregated into per unit costs fixed costs per period, and variable costs as a proportion of revenue. Capital expenditures will usually be allocated separately, and depending on the purpose, a portion may be regularly allocated to expenses as depreciation and amortization and seen as a _____ per period, or the entire amount may be considered upfront fixed costs.
   a. Fixed cost0
   c. Undefined
   b. Thing
   d. Undefined

45. _____ is the extra revenue that an additional unit of product will bring a firm. It can also be described as the change in total revenue/change in number of units sold.
   a. Marginal revenue0
   c. Undefined
   b. Thing
   d. Undefined

46. _____ is a business term for the amount of money that a company receives from its activities in a given period, mostly from sales of products and/or services to customers
   a. Revenue0
   c. Undefined
   b. Thing
   d. Undefined

Chapter 6. Integration and Its Applications

47. In economics, supply and _____ describe market relations between prospective sellers and buyers of a good.
a. Demand0
b. Thing
c. Undefined
d. Undefined

48. _____, from Latin meaning "to make progress", is defined in two different ways. Pure economic _____ is the increase in wealth that an investor has from making an investment, taking into consideration all costs associated with that investment including the opportunity cost of capital.
a. Profit0
b. Thing
c. Undefined
d. Undefined

49. In mathematics, an _____, mean, or central tendency of a data set refers to a measure of the "middle" or "expected" value of the data set.
a. Concept
b. Average0
c. Undefined
d. Undefined

50. _____ are expenses whose total does not change in proportion to the activity of a business, within the relevant time period or scale of production
a. Thing
b. Fixed costs0
c. Undefined
d. Undefined

51. In sociology and biology a _____ is the collection of people or organisms of a particular species living in a given geographic area or space, usually measured by a census.
a. Population0
b. Thing
c. Undefined
d. Undefined

52. _____ is change in population over time, and can be quantified as the change in the number of individuals in a population per unit time.
a. Thing
b. Population growth0
c. Undefined
d. Undefined

53. The word _____ comes from the Latin word linearis, which means created by lines.
a. Linear0
b. Thing
c. Undefined
d. Undefined

54. In elementary algebra, an _____ is a set that contains every real number between two indicated numbers and may contain the two numbers themselves.
a. Interval0
b. Thing
c. Undefined
d. Undefined

55. A frame of _____ is a particular perspective from which the universe is observed.
a. Reference0
b. Thing
c. Undefined
d. Undefined

56. In mathematics, _____ is the decomposition of an object into a product of other objects, or factors, which when multiplied together give the original.

Chapter 6. Integration and Its Applications

    a. Factoring0
    c. Undefined
    b. Thing
    d. Undefined

57. A _____ is a quantity that denotes the proportional amount or magnitude of one quantity relative to another.
    a. Thing
    c. Undefined
    b. Ratio0
    d. Undefined

58. _____ is a branch of mathematics concerning the study of structure, relation and quantity.
    a. Algebra0
    c. Undefined
    b. Concept
    d. Undefined

59. In mathematics, two quantities are called _____ if they vary in such a way that one of the quantities is a constant multiple of the other, or equivalently if they have a constant ratio.
    a. Thing
    c. Undefined
    b. Proportional0
    d. Undefined

60. In plane geometry, a _____ is a polygon with four equal sides, four right angles, and parallel opposite sides. In algebra, the _____ of a number is that number multiplied by itself.
    a. Square0
    c. Undefined
    b. Thing
    d. Undefined

61. _____ is a kind of property which exists as magnitude or multitude. It is among the basic classes of things along with quality, substance, change, and relation.
    a. Thing
    c. Undefined
    b. Amount0
    d. Undefined

62. _____ usually refers to money in the form of liquid currency, such as banknotes or coins.
    a. Thing
    c. Undefined
    b. Cash0
    d. Undefined

63. In mathematics, _____ growth occurs when the growth rate of a function is always proportional to the function's current size.
    a. Exponential0
    c. Undefined
    b. Thing
    d. Undefined

64. _____ is one of the most important functions in mathematics. A function commonly used to study growth and decay
    a. Exponential function0
    c. Undefined
    b. Thing
    d. Undefined

65. _____ is the chance that something is likely to happen or be the case.
    a. Probability0
    c. Undefined
    b. Thing
    d. Undefined

66. In mathematics, an _____ number is a complex number whose square is a negative real number. They were defined in 1572 by Rafael Bombelli.

Chapter 6. Integration and Its Applications

a. Imaginary0
b. Thing
c. Undefined
d. Undefined

67. In mathematics, the _____ i (or sometimes the Latin j or the Greek iota, see below) allows the real number system R to be extended to the complex number system C. Its precise definition is dependent upon the particular method of extension.
    a. Thing
    b. Imaginary unit0
    c. Undefined
    d. Undefined

68. In mathematics, the _____ (or modulus) of a real number is its numerical value without regard to its sign.
    a. Thing
    b. Absolute value0
    c. Undefined
    d. Undefined

69. In arithmetic, _____ is a procedure for calculating the division of one integer, called the dividend, by another integer called the divisor, to produce a result called the quotient.
    a. Thing
    b. Long division0
    c. Undefined
    d. Undefined

70. In linear algebra, the _____ of an n-by-n square matrix A is defined to be the sum of the elements on the main diagonal of A,
    a. Thing
    b. Trace0
    c. Undefined
    d. Undefined

71. In geographic information systems, a _____ comprises an entity with a geographic location, typically determined by points, arcs, or polygons. Carriageways and cadastres exemplify _____ data.
    a. Thing
    b. Feature0
    c. Undefined
    d. Undefined

72. A _____ is an individual or household that purchases and uses goods and services generated within the economy.
    a. Consumer0
    b. Thing
    c. Undefined
    d. Undefined

73. In Graph theory, a _____ is a digraph with weighted edges.
    a. Network0
    b. Concept
    c. Undefined
    d. Undefined

74. In common philosophical language, a proposition or _____, is the content of an assertion, that is, it is true-or-false and defined by the meaning of a particular piece of language.
    a. Concept
    b. Statement0
    c. Undefined
    d. Undefined

75. _____ is an extension of the concept of a sum.
    a. Thing
    b. Definite integral0
    c. Undefined
    d. Undefined

Chapter 6. Integration and Its Applications

76. In mathematics, a _____ is a statement that can be proved on the basis of explicitly stated or previously agreed assumptions.
    a. Thing
    b. Theorem0
    c. Undefined
    d. Undefined

77. In number theory, the _____ of arithmetic (or unique factorization theorem) states that every natural number greater than 1 can be written as a unique product of prime numbers.
    a. Concept
    b. Fundamental theorem0
    c. Undefined
    d. Undefined

78. _____ of calculus is the statement that the two central operations of calculus, differentiation and integration, are inverse operations: if a continuous function is first integrated and then differentiated, the original function is retrieved.
    a. Fundamental Theorem of Calculus0
    b. Thing
    c. Undefined
    d. Undefined

79. _____ is the use of marginal concepts within economics. Marginal concepts include marginal cost, marginal productivity and marginal utility, the law of diminishing rates of substitution, and the law of diminishing marginal utility.
    a. Thing
    b. Marginal analysis0
    c. Undefined
    d. Undefined

80. In mathematical analysis and related areas of mathematics, a set is called _____, if it is, in a certain sense, of finite size.
    a. Bounded0
    b. Thing
    c. Undefined
    d. Undefined

81. A _____ is one of the basic shapes of geometry: a polygon with three vertices and three sides which are straight line segments.
    a. Triangle0
    b. Thing
    c. Undefined
    d. Undefined

82. A _____ function is a function for which, intuitively, small changes in the input result in small changes in the output.
    a. Continuous0
    b. Event
    c. Undefined
    d. Undefined

83. The _____ integers are all the integers from zero on upwards.
    a. Thing
    b. Nonnegative0
    c. Undefined
    d. Undefined

84. In mathematics, a _____ is a countable collection of open covers of a topological space that satisfies certain separation axioms.
    a. Development0
    b. Thing
    c. Undefined
    d. Undefined

85. In business, particularly accounting, a _____ is the time intervals that the accounts, statement, payments, or other calculations cover.

Chapter 6. Integration and Its Applications

   a. Period0
   c. Undefined
   b. Thing
   d. Undefined

86. In mathematics, the _____ of a coordinate system is the point where the axes of the system intersect.
   a. Thing
   c. Undefined
   b. Origin0
   d. Undefined

87. In mathematics, a _____ is an ordered list of objects. Like a set, it contains members, also called elements or terms, and the number of terms is called the length of the _____. Unlike a set, order matters, and the exact same elements can appear multiple times at different positions in the _____.
   a. Thing
   c. Undefined
   b. Sequence0
   d. Undefined

88. In mathematics, a _____ function in the sense of algebraic geometry is an everywhere-defined, polynomial function on an algebraic variety V with values in the field K over which V is defined.
   a. Thing
   c. Undefined
   b. Regular0
   d. Undefined

89. _____ is the income from capital investment paid in a series of regular payments.
   a. Annuity0
   c. Undefined
   b. Thing
   d. Undefined

90. _____ is the fee paid on borrowed money.
   a. Interest0
   c. Undefined
   b. Thing
   d. Undefined

91. An _____ is the fee paid on borrow money.
   a. Interest rate0
   c. Undefined
   b. Concept
   d. Undefined

92. _____ is a retirement plan account that provides some tax advantages for retirement savings in the United States.
   a. Individual Retirement Account0
   c. Undefined
   b. Thing
   d. Undefined

93. _____ or investing is a term with several closely-related meanings in business management, finance and economics, related to saving or deferring consumption.
   a. Investment0
   c. Undefined
   b. Thing
   d. Undefined

94. _____ is a term used in accounting, economics and finance with reference to the fact that assets with finite lives lose value over time.
   a. Depreciation0
   c. Undefined
   b. Thing
   d. Undefined

95. A _____ are accounts maintained by commercial banks, savings and loan associations, credit unions, and mutual savings banks that pay interest but can not be used directly as money by, for example, writing a cheque.

Chapter 6. Integration and Its Applications

a. Savings account0
b. Thing
c. Undefined
d. Undefined

96. _____ interest refers to the fact that whenever interest is calculated, it is based not only on the original principal, but also on any unpaid interest that has been added to the principal.
a. Thing
b. Compound0
c. Undefined
d. Undefined

97. _____ refers to the fact that whenever interest is calculated, it is based not only on the original principal, but also on any unpaid interest that has been added to the principal. The more frequently interest is compounded, the faster the balance grows.
a. Concept
b. Compound interest0
c. Undefined
d. Undefined

98. In geometry, the _____ of an object is a point in some sense in the middle of the object.
a. Center0
b. Thing
c. Undefined
d. Undefined

99. In classical geometry, a _____ of a circle or sphere is any line segment from its center to its boundary. By extension, the _____ of a circle or sphere is the length of any such segment. The _____ is half the diameter. In science and engineering the term _____ of curvature is commonly used as a synonym for _____.
a. Thing
b. Radius0
c. Undefined
d. Undefined

100. _____ is a synonym for information.
a. Thing
b. Data0
c. Undefined
d. Undefined

101. In geometry, _____ lines are two lines that share one or more common points.
a. Intersecting0
b. Thing
c. Undefined
d. Undefined

102. In mathematics, the _____ of two sets A and B is the set that contains all elements of A that also belong to B (or equivalently, all elements of B that also belong to A), but no other elements.
a. Intersection0
b. Thing
c. Undefined
d. Undefined

103. Any point where a graph makes contact with an coordinate axis is called an _____ of the graph
a. Thing
b. Intercept0
c. Undefined
d. Undefined

104. _____ is used in economics for several related quantities
a. Thing
b. Producer surplus0
c. Undefined
d. Undefined

Chapter 6. Integration and Its Applications

105. In economics, economic _____ is simply a state of the world where economic forces are balanced and in the absence of external influences the values of economic variables will not change.
   a. Equilibrium0
   b. Thing
   c. Undefined
   d. Undefined

106. In astronomy, geography, geometry and related sciences and contexts, a plane is said to be _____ at a given point if it is locally perpendicular to the gradient of the gravity field, i.e., with the direction of the gravitational force at that point.
   a. Thing
   b. Horizontal0
   c. Undefined
   d. Undefined

107. _____ traditionally refers to the statistical process of determining comparable scores on different forms of an exam
   a. Thing
   b. Equating0
   c. Undefined
   d. Undefined

108. _____ is a state located in the southern and southwestern regions of the United States of America.
   a. Thing
   b. Texas0
   c. Undefined
   d. Undefined

109. In geometry, a _____ is a special kind of point, usually a corner of a polygon, polyhedron, or higher dimensional polytope. In the geometry of curves a _____ is a point of where the first derivative of curvature is zero. In graph theory, a _____ is the fundamental unit out of which graphs are formed
   a. Thing
   b. Vertex0
   c. Undefined
   d. Undefined

110. The _____ of a ring R is defined to be the smallest positive integer n such that $n\,a = 0$, for all a in R.
   a. Characteristic0
   b. Thing
   c. Undefined
   d. Undefined

111. In epidemiology, an _____ is a disease that appears as new cases in a given human population, during a given period, at a rate that substantially exceeds with is "expected," based on recent experience.
   a. Epidemic0
   b. Thing
   c. Undefined
   d. Undefined

112. _____ is the level of functional and/or metabolic efficiency of an organism at both the micro level.
   a. Thing
   b. Health0
   c. Undefined
   d. Undefined

113. _____ is the production of food, feed, fiber, fuel and other goods by the systematic raizing of plants and animals.
   a. Thing
   b. Agriculture0
   c. Undefined
   d. Undefined

114. _____ is the application of tools and a processing medium to the transformation of raw materials into finished goods for sale.

Chapter 6. Integration and Its Applications

a. Thing
b. Manufacturing0
c. Undefined
d. Undefined

115. In mathematics, the concept of a _____ tries to capture the intuitive idea of a geometrical one-dimensional and continuous object. A simple example is the circle.
a. Curve0
b. Thing
c. Undefined
d. Undefined

116. In mathematics, _____ are the intuitive idea of a geometrical one-dimensional and continuous object.
a. Curves0
b. Thing
c. Undefined
d. Undefined

117. In mathematical analysis, _____ are objects which generalize functions and probability distributions.
a. Distribution0
b. Thing
c. Undefined
d. Undefined

118. _____ is a way of expressing a number as a fraction of 100 per cent meaning "per hundred".
a. Percent0
b. Thing
c. Undefined
d. Undefined

119. In mathematics, an _____ is a statement about the relative size or order of two objects.
a. Thing
b. Inequality0
c. Undefined
d. Undefined

120. _____ is the middle point of a line segment.
a. Thing
b. Midpoint0
c. Undefined
d. Undefined

121. In geometry, a _____ is defined as a quadrilateral where all four of its angles are right angles.
a. Rectangle0
b. Thing
c. Undefined
d. Undefined

122. _____ are any documents that aim to streamline particular processes according to a set routine.
a. Guidelines0
b. Thing
c. Undefined
d. Undefined

123. _____ the American term is a way to approximately calculate the definite integral
a. Thing
b. Trapezoidal Rule0
c. Undefined
d. Undefined

124. _____ is the transport of people on a trip/journey or the process or time involved in a person or object moving from one location to another.
a. Thing
b. Travel0
c. Undefined
d. Undefined

Chapter 6. Integration and Its Applications

125. The _____ of a solid object is the three-dimensional concept of how much space it occupies, often quantified numerically.
   a. Volume0
   b. Thing
   c. Undefined
   d. Undefined

126. In mathematics, _____ geometry was the traditional name for the geometry of three-dimensional Euclidean space — for practical purposes the kind of space we live in.
   a. Thing
   b. Solid0
   c. Undefined
   d. Undefined

127. _____ is a means of calculating the volume of a solid of revolution, when integrating along the axis of revolution. This method models the generated 3 dimensional shape as a "stack" of an infinite number of disks of infinitesimal thickness.
   a. Thing
   b. Disk method0
   c. Undefined
   d. Undefined

128. An _____ is a straight line around which a geometric figure can be rotated.
   a. Thing
   b. Axis0
   c. Undefined
   d. Undefined

129. In geometry, a line _____ is a part of a line that is bounded by two end points, and contains every point on the line between its end points.
   a. Concept
   b. Segment0
   c. Undefined
   d. Undefined

130. A _____ is a part of a line that is bounded by two end points, and contains every point on the line between its end points.
   a. Line segment0
   b. Thing
   c. Undefined
   d. Undefined

131. A _____ is a three-dimensional geometric shape formed by straight lines through a fixed point (vertex) to the points of a fixed curve (directrix)
   a. Cone0
   b. Concept
   c. Undefined
   d. Undefined

132. _____ is a three-dimensional geometric shape formed by straight lines through a fixed point vertex to the points of a fixed curve directrix.
   a. Thing
   b. Right circular cone0
   c. Undefined
   d. Undefined

133. In mathematics, an _____ .
   a. Ellipse0
   b. Thing
   c. Undefined
   d. Undefined

Chapter 6. Integration and Its Applications

134. In mathematics, a _____ is the set of all points in three-dimensional space (R^3) which are at distance r from a fixed point of that space, where r is a positive real number called the radius of the _____. The fixed point is called the center or centre, and is not part of the _____ itself.
   a. Thing
   b. Sphere0
   c. Undefined
   d. Undefined

135. The metre (or _____, see spelling differences) is a measure of length. It is the basic unit of length in the metric system and in the International System of Units (SI), used around the world for general and scientific purposes.
   a. Meter0
   b. Concept
   c. Undefined
   d. Undefined

136. In mathematics, the _____ f is the collection of all ordered pairs . In particular, graph means the graphical representation of this collection, in the form of a curve or surface, together with axes, etc. Graphing on a Cartesian plane is sometimes referred to as curve sketching.
   a. Graph of a function0
   b. Thing
   c. Undefined
   d. Undefined

137. _____ are functions which satisfy particular symmetry relations, with respect to taking additive inverses.
   a. Even function0
   b. Thing
   c. Undefined
   d. Undefined

138. In abstract algebra, _____ consists of sets with binary operations that satisfy certain axioms.
   a. Grouping0
   b. Thing
   c. Undefined
   d. Undefined

139. _____ are objects, characters, or other concrete representations of ideas, concepts, or other abstractions.
   a. Thing
   b. Symbols0
   c. Undefined
   d. Undefined

140. _____, in law and economics, is a form of risk management primarily used to hedge against the risk of a contingent loss.
   a. Insurance0
   b. Thing
   c. Undefined
   d. Undefined

141. The _____ consists of an inhalation and an exhalation.
   a. Respiratory cycle0
   b. Thing
   c. Undefined
   d. Undefined

142. In statistics, a _____ measure is one which is measuring what is supposed to measure.
   a. Thing
   b. Valid0
   c. Undefined
   d. Undefined

143. In mathematics, the _____ of a function is the set of all "output" values produced by that function. Given a function $f : A \to B$, the _____ of f, is defined to be the set $\{x \in B : x = f(a)$ for some $a \in A\}$.

a. Range0
c. Undefined

b. Thing
d. Undefined

Chapter 7. Techniques of Integration

1. The _____ of a function is an extension of the concept of a sum, and are identified or found through the use of integration.
   - a. Thing
   - b. Integral0
   - c. Undefined
   - d. Undefined

2. _____ is an extension of the concept of a sum.
   - a. Thing
   - b. Definite integral0
   - c. Undefined
   - d. Undefined

3. _____ is a process of combining or accumulating. It may also refer to:
   - a. Thing
   - b. Integration0
   - c. Undefined
   - d. Undefined

4. _____, a field in mathematics, is the study of how functions change when their inputs change. The primary object of study in _____ is the derivative.
   - a. Thing
   - b. Differential calculus0
   - c. Undefined
   - d. Undefined

5. In mathematics, _____ growth occurs when the growth rate of a function is always proportional to the function's current size.
   - a. Thing
   - b. Exponential0
   - c. Undefined
   - d. Undefined

6. The _____, the average in everyday English, which is also called the arithmetic _____ (and is distinguished from the geometric _____ or harmonic _____). The average is also called the sample _____. The expected value of a random variable, which is also called the population _____.
   - a. Mean0
   - b. Thing
   - c. Undefined
   - d. Undefined

7. The mathematical concept of a _____ expresses the intuitive idea of deterministic dependence between two quantities, one of which is viewed as primary and the other as secondary. A _____ then is a way to associate a unique output for each input of a specified type, for example, a real number or an element of a given set.
   - a. Function0
   - b. Thing
   - c. Undefined
   - d. Undefined

8. _____ has many meanings, most of which simply .
   - a. Thing
   - b. Power0
   - c. Undefined
   - d. Undefined

9. _____ is a method for differentiating expressions involving exponentiation the power operation.
   - a. Power rule0
   - b. Thing
   - c. Undefined
   - d. Undefined

10. In mathematics and the mathematical sciences, a _____ is a fixed, but possibly unspecified, value. This is in contrast to a variable, which is not fixed.

a. Constant0 b. Thing
c. Undefined d. Undefined

11. _____ the expected value of a random variable displays the average or central value of the variable. It is a summary value of the distribution of the variable.
   a. Thing b. Determining0
   c. Undefined d. Undefined

12. _____ is a tool for finding antiderivatives and integrals. Using the fundamental theorem of calculus often requires finding an antiderivative. For this and other reasons, this rule is a relatively important tool for mathematicians. It is the counterpart to the chain rule of differentiation.
   a. Integration by substitution0 b. Thing
   c. Undefined d. Undefined

13. An _____ of a function f is a function F whose derivative is equal to f, i.e., F' = f.
   a. Thing b. Antiderivative0
   c. Undefined d. Undefined

14. _____ are any documents that aim to streamline particular processes according to a set routine.
   a. Guidelines0 b. Thing
   c. Undefined d. Undefined

15. _____ is a function that extends the concept of an ordinary sum
   a. Thing b. Integrand0
   c. Undefined d. Undefined

16. A _____ is a symbolic representation denoting a quantity or expression. It often represents an "unknown" quantity that has the potential to change.
   a. Variable0 b. Thing
   c. Undefined d. Undefined

17. A _____ is a negotiable instrument instructing a financial institution to pay a specific amount of a specific currency from a specific demand account held in the maker/depositor's name with that institution. Both the maker and payee may be natural persons or legal entities.
   a. Thing b. Check0
   c. Undefined d. Undefined

18. _____ is the chance that something is likely to happen or be the case.
   a. Probability0 b. Thing
   c. Undefined d. Undefined

19. _____ is a function that represents a probability distribution in terms of integrals.
   a. Probability density function0 b. Thing
   c. Undefined d. Undefined

20. _____ is mass m per unit volume V.

a. Thing
b. Density0
c. Undefined
d. Undefined

21. In the scientific method, an _____ (Latin: ex-+-periri, "of (or from) trying"), is a set of actions and observations, performed in the context of solving a particular problem or question, in order to support or falsify a hypothesis or research concerning phenomena.
   a. Experiment0
   b. Thing
   c. Undefined
   d. Undefined

22. _____ is a way of expressing a number as a fraction of 100 per cent meaning "per hundred".
   a. Thing
   b. Percent0
   c. Undefined
   d. Undefined

23. An _____ is a combination of numbers, operators, grouping symbols and/or free variables and bound variables arranged in a meaningful way which can be evaluated..
   a. Expression0
   b. Thing
   c. Undefined
   d. Undefined

24. _____ are the basic objects of study in graph theory. Informally speaking, a graph is a set of objects called points, nodes, or vertices connected by links called lines or edges.
   a. Thing
   b. Graphs0
   c. Undefined
   d. Undefined

25. In mathematical analysis and related areas of mathematics, a set is called _____, if it is, in a certain sense, of finite size.
   a. Thing
   b. Bounded0
   c. Undefined
   d. Undefined

26. The _____ of a solid object is the three-dimensional concept of how much space it occupies, often quantified numerically.
   a. Thing
   b. Volume0
   c. Undefined
   d. Undefined

27. In mathematics, _____ geometry was the traditional name for the geometry of three-dimensional Euclidean space — for practical purposes the kind of space we live in.
   a. Solid0
   b. Thing
   c. Undefined
   d. Undefined

28. In mathematics, a _____ is the result of multiplying, or an expression that identifies factors to be multiplied.
   a. Product0
   b. Thing
   c. Undefined
   d. Undefined

29. _____ is a business term for the amount of money that a company receives from its activities in a given period, mostly from sales of products and/or services to customers

a. Thing
b. Revenue0
c. Undefined
d. Undefined

30. Deductive _____ is the kind of _____ in which the conclusion is necessitated by, or reached from, previously known facts (the premises).
a. Thing
b. Reasoning0
c. Undefined
d. Undefined

31. In mathematics, an _____, mean, or central tendency of a data set refers to a measure of the "middle" or "expected" value of the data set.
a. Concept
b. Average0
c. Undefined
d. Undefined

32. _____ is a kind of property which exists as magnitude or multitude. It is among the basic classes of things along with quality, substance, change, and relation.
a. Thing
b. Amount0
c. Undefined
d. Undefined

33. In elementary algebra, an _____ is a set that contains every real number between two indicated numbers and may contain the two numbers themselves.
a. Thing
b. Interval0
c. Undefined
d. Undefined

34. _____ of a single or multiple future payments is the nominal amounts of money to change hands at some future date, discounted to account for the time value of money, and other factors such as investment risk.
a. Thing
b. Present value0
c. Undefined
d. Undefined

35. The _____ governs the differentiation of products of differentiable functions.
a. Thing
b. Product rule0
c. Undefined
d. Undefined

36. The _____ is a measurement of how a function changes when the values of its inputs change.
a. Thing
b. Derivative0
c. Undefined
d. Undefined

37. In mathematics, factorization (British English: factorisation) or factoring is the decomposition of an object (for example, a number, a polynomial, or a matrix) into a product of other objects, or _____, which when multiplied together give the original.
a. Factors0
b. Thing
c. Undefined
d. Undefined

38. In mainstream economics, the word _____ refers to a general rise in prices measured against a standard level of purchasing power.

a. Thing
b. Inflation0
c. Undefined
d. Undefined

39. A _____ function is a function for which, intuitively, small changes in the input result in small changes in the output.
a. Continuous0
b. Event
c. Undefined
d. Undefined

40. A _____ is a special kind of ratio, indicating a relationship between two measurements with different units, such as miles to gallons or cents to pounds.
a. Thing
b. Rate0
c. Undefined
d. Undefined

41. _____ is the fee paid on borrowed money.
a. Interest0
b. Thing
c. Undefined
d. Undefined

42. An _____ is the fee paid on borrow money.
a. Concept
b. Interest rate0
c. Undefined
d. Undefined

43. The _____ is a popular form of gambling which involves the drawing of lots for a prize. Some governments forbid it, while others endorse it to the extent of organizign a national _____
a. Lottery0
b. Thing
c. Undefined
d. Undefined

44. _____ is the income from capital investment paid in a series of regular payments.
a. Thing
b. Annuity0
c. Undefined
d. Undefined

45. The _____ of measurement are a globally standardized and modernized form of the metric system.
a. Units0
b. Thing
c. Undefined
d. Undefined

46. _____ is the application of tools and a processing medium to the transformation of raw materials into finished goods for sale.
a. Thing
b. Manufacturing0
c. Undefined
d. Undefined

47. In economics, supply and _____ describe market relations between prospective sellers and buyers of a good.
a. Demand0
b. Thing
c. Undefined
d. Undefined

48. In business, particularly accounting, a _____ is the time intervals that the accounts, statement, payments, or other calculations cover.

a. Period0
b. Thing
c. Undefined
d. Undefined

49. In Euclidean geometry, a uniform _____ is a linear transformation that enlargers or diminishes objects, and whose _____ factor is the same in all directions. This is also called homothethy.
   a. Scale0
   b. Thing
   c. Undefined
   d. Undefined

50. _____ measures the nominal future sum of money that a given sum of money is "worth" at a specified time in the future assuming a certain interest rate; this value does not include corrections for inflation or other factors that affect the true value of money in the future.
   a. Thing
   b. Future value0
   c. Undefined
   d. Undefined

51. _____ or investing is a term with several closely-related meanings in business management, finance and economics, related to saving or deferring consumption.
   a. Investment0
   b. Thing
   c. Undefined
   d. Undefined

52. _____ studies and addresses the ways in which individuals, businesses, and organizations raise, allocate, and use monetary resources over time, taking into account the risks entailed in their projects
   a. Finance0
   b. Thing
   c. Undefined
   d. Undefined

53. _____ is the middle point of a line segment.
   a. Midpoint0
   b. Thing
   c. Undefined
   d. Undefined

54. In algebra, the _____ decomposition or _____ expansion is used to reduce the degree of either the numerator or the denominator of a rational function.
   a. Thing
   b. Partial fraction0
   c. Undefined
   d. Undefined

55. A _____ fraction is a fraction in which the absolute value of the numerator is less than the denominator--hence, the absolute value of the fraction is less than 1.
   a. Thing
   b. Proper0
   c. Undefined
   d. Undefined

56. In mathematics, a _____ number is a number which can be expressed as a ratio of two integers. Non-integer _____ numbers (commonly called fractions) are usually written as the vulgar fraction a / b, where b is not zero.
   a. Rational0
   b. Thing
   c. Undefined
   d. Undefined

57. In mathematics, a _____ is any function which can be written as the ratio of two polynomial functions.

Chapter 7. Techniques of Integration

a. Rational function0   b. Thing
c. Undefined   d. Undefined

58. A _____ is the result of the addition of a set of numbers. The numbers may be natural numbers, complex numbers, matrices, or still more complicated objects. An infinite _____ is a subtle procedure known as a series.
   a. Thing
   b. Sum0
   c. Undefined
   d. Undefined

59. _____ refers to the reduction of the body of a formerly living organism into simpler forms of matter.
   a. Decomposing0
   b. Thing
   c. Undefined
   d. Undefined

60. The word _____ comes from the Latin word linearis, which means created by lines.
   a. Linear0
   b. Thing
   c. Undefined
   d. Undefined

61. A _____ is a numeral used to indicate a count. The most common use of the word today is to name the part of a fraction that tells the number or count of equal parts.
   a. Thing
   b. Numerator0
   c. Undefined
   d. Undefined

62. In mathematics, there are several meanings of _____ depending on the subject.
   a. Thing
   b. Degree0
   c. Undefined
   d. Undefined

63. A _____ is the part of a fraction that tells how many equal parts make up a whole, and which is used in the name of the fraction: "halves", "thirds", "fourths" or "quarters", "fifths" and so on.
   a. Concept
   b. Denominator0
   c. Undefined
   d. Undefined

64. In mathematics, _____ is the decomposition of an object into a product of other objects, or factors, which when multiplied together give the original.
   a. Factoring0
   b. Thing
   c. Undefined
   d. Undefined

65. In mathematics, _____ occurs when the growth rate of a function is always proportional to the function's current size.
   a. Exponential growth0
   b. Thing
   c. Undefined
   d. Undefined

66. An _____ is a straight line or curve A to which another curve B approaches closer and closer as one moves along it. As one moves along B, the space between it and the _____ A becomes smaller and smaller, and can in fact be made as small as one could wish by going far enough along. A curve may or may not touch or cross its _____. In fact, the curve may intersect the _____ an infinite number of times.

108 Chapter 7. Techniques of Integration

    a. Asymptote0
    c. Undefined
    b. Thing
    d. Undefined

67. In astronomy, geography, geometry and related sciences and contexts, a plane is said to be _____ at a given point if it is locally perpendicular to the gradient of the gravity field, i.e., with the direction of the gravitational force at that point.
    a. Horizontal0
    c. Undefined
    b. Thing
    d. Undefined

68. In sociology and biology a _____ is the collection of people or organisms of a particular species living in a given geographic area or space, usually measured by a census.
    a. Thing
    c. Undefined
    b. Population0
    d. Undefined

69. The payment of _____ as remuneration for services rendered or products sold is a common way to reward sales people.
    a. Commission0
    c. Undefined
    b. Thing
    d. Undefined

70. In mathematics, two quantities are called _____ if they vary in such a way that one of the quantities is a constant multiple of the other, or equivalently if they have a constant ratio.
    a. Proportional0
    c. Undefined
    b. Thing
    d. Undefined

71. In mathematics, the conjugate _____ or adjoint matrix of an m-by-n matrix A with complex entries is the n-by-m matrix A* obtained from A by taking the transpose and then taking the complex conjugate of each entry.
    a. Pairs0
    c. Undefined
    b. Thing
    d. Undefined

72. _____ refers to all non-domesticated plants, animals, and other organisms.
    a. Wildlife0
    c. Undefined
    b. Thing
    d. Undefined

73. In mathematics, a _____ is an expression that is constructed from one or more variables and constants, using only the operations of addition, subtraction, multiplication, and constant positive whole number exponents. is a _____. Note in particular that division by an expression containing a variable is not in general allowed in polynomials. [1]
    a. Thing
    c. Undefined
    b. Polynomial0
    d. Undefined

74. A _____ is a large group of animals. The term is usually applied to mammals, particularly ungulates. Other terms are used for similar phenomena in other types of animal.
    a. Herd0
    c. Undefined
    b. Thing
    d. Undefined

75. _____ is the ability to hold, receive or absorb, or a measure thereof, similar to the concept of volume.

Chapter 7. Techniques of Integration

a. Capacity0
b. Concept
c. Undefined
d. Undefined

76. _____ is a special mathematical relationship between two quantities. Two quantities are called proportional if they vary in such a way that one of the quantities is a constant multiple of the other, or equivalently if they have a constant ratio.
   a. Thing
   b. Proportionality0
   c. Undefined
   d. Undefined

77. In calculus, the indefinite integral of a given function i.e. the set of all antiderivatives of the function is always written with a constant, the _____.
   a. Thing
   b. Constant of integration0
   c. Undefined
   d. Undefined

78. In epidemiology, an _____ is a disease that appears as new cases in a given human population, during a given period, at a rate that substantially exceeds with is "expected," based on recent experience.
   a. Thing
   b. Epidemic0
   c. Undefined
   d. Undefined

79. _____ is the level of functional and/or metabolic efficiency of an organism at both the micro level.
   a. Thing
   b. Health0
   c. Undefined
   d. Undefined

80. Acid _____ ratio measures the ability of a company to use its near cash or quick assets to immediately extinguish its current liabilities.
   a. Thing
   b. Test0
   c. Undefined
   d. Undefined

81. _____ Any process by which a specified characteristic usually amplitude of the output of a device is prevented from exceeding a predetermined value.
   a. Thing
   b. Limiting0
   c. Undefined
   d. Undefined

82. In mathematics, the concept of a _____ tries to capture the intuitive idea of a geometrical one-dimensional and continuous object. A simple example is the circle.
   a. Thing
   b. Curve0
   c. Undefined
   d. Undefined

83. In mathematics, _____ are the intuitive idea of a geometrical one-dimensional and continuous object.
   a. Curves0
   b. Thing
   c. Undefined
   d. Undefined

84. _____ is change in population over time, and can be quantified as the change in the number of individuals in a population per unit time.

a. Thing
b. Population growth0
c. Undefined
d. Undefined

85. _____ are procedures that allow people to exchange information by one of several methods.
a. Thing
b. Communications0
c. Undefined
d. Undefined

86. In plane geometry, a _____ is a polygon with four equal sides, four right angles, and parallel opposite sides. In algebra, the _____ of a number is that number multiplied by itself.
a. Square0
b. Thing
c. Undefined
d. Undefined

87. _____ is a technique used in algebra to solve quadratic equations, in analytic geometry for determining the shapes of graphs, and in calculus for computing integrals, including, but hardly limited to, the integrals that define Laplace transforms. The essential objective is to reduce a quadratic polynomial in a variable in an equation or expression to a squared polynomial of linear order. This can reduce an equation or integral to one that is more easily solved or evaluated.
a. Completing the square0
b. Thing
c. Undefined
d. Undefined

88. In mathematics, _____ refers to the rewriting of an expression into a simpler form.
a. Reduction0
b. Thing
c. Undefined
d. Undefined

89. The easiest _____ prime numbers resides in the use of the Sieve of Eratosthenes, an algorithm that discovers all prime numbers to a specified integer.
a. Method for finding0
b. Thing
c. Undefined
d. Undefined

90. In combinatorial mathematics, a _____ is an un-ordered collection of unique elements.
a. Combination0
b. Concept
c. Undefined
d. Undefined

91. _____ is a branch of mathematics concerning the study of structure, relation and quantity.
a. Algebra0
b. Concept
c. Undefined
d. Undefined

92. In mathematics the _____ refers to the identity: $a^2 - b^2 = (a+b)(a-b)$
a. Difference of two squares0
b. Thing
c. Undefined
d. Undefined

93. _____ is the extra revenue that an additional unit of product will bring a firm. It can also be described as the change in total revenue/change in number of units sold.
a. Thing
b. Marginal revenue0
c. Undefined
d. Undefined

94. _____ is used in economics for several related quantities

Chapter 7. Techniques of Integration 111

a. Thing
b. Producer surplus0
c. Undefined
d. Undefined

95. A _____ is an individual or household that purchases and uses goods and services generated within the economy.
a. Consumer0
b. Thing
c. Undefined
d. Undefined

96. In topology and related areas of mathematics a _____ or Moore-Smith sequence is a generalization of a sequence, intended to unify the various notions of limit and generalize them to arbitrary topological spaces.
a. Thing
b. Net0
c. Undefined
d. Undefined

97. _____ is an accounting term which is commonly used in business.
a. Net profit0
b. Thing
c. Undefined
d. Undefined

98. _____, from Latin meaning "to make progress", is defined in two different ways. Pure economic _____ is the increase in wealth that an investor has from making an investment, taking into consideration all costs associated with that investment including the opportunity cost of capital.
a. Profit0
b. Thing
c. Undefined
d. Undefined

99. _____ the American term is a way to approximately calculate the definite integral
a. Trapezoidal Rule0
b. Thing
c. Undefined
d. Undefined

100. _____ constitutes a broad family of algorithms for calculating the numerical value of a definite integral, and by extension, the term is also sometimes used to describe the numerical solution of differential equations.
a. Thing
b. Numerical integration0
c. Undefined
d. Undefined

101. A _____ is a quadrilateral, which is defined as a shape with four sides, which has a pair of parallel sides.
a. Trapezoid0
b. Thing
c. Undefined
d. Undefined

102. In statistics, a _____ measure is one which is measuring what is supposed to measure.
a. Valid0
b. Thing
c. Undefined
d. Undefined

103. The _____ integers are all the integers from zero on upwards.
a. Thing
b. Nonnegative0
c. Undefined
d. Undefined

104. In mathematics, a _____ is a countable collection of open covers of a topological space that satisfies certain separation axioms.

Chapter 7. Techniques of Integration

a. Development0
b. Thing
c. Undefined
d. Undefined

105. In mathematics, a _____ is a constant multiplicative factor of a certain object. The object can be such things as a variable, a vector, a function, etc. For example, the _____ of $9x^2$ is 9.
   a. Coefficient0
   b. Thing
   c. Undefined
   d. Undefined

106. In geometry, an _____ is a point at which a line segment or ray terminates.
   a. Endpoint0
   b. Thing
   c. Undefined
   d. Undefined

107. In mathematics, a _____ is a statement that can be proved on the basis of explicitly stated or previously agreed assumptions.
   a. Thing
   b. Theorem0
   c. Undefined
   d. Undefined

108. _____ is a mathematical subject that includes the study of limits, derivatives, integrals, and power series and constitutes a major part of modern university curriculum.
   a. Calculus0
   b. Thing
   c. Undefined
   d. Undefined

109. In number theory, the _____ of arithmetic (or unique factorization theorem) states that every natural number greater than 1 can be written as a unique product of prime numbers.
   a. Fundamental theorem0
   b. Concept
   c. Undefined
   d. Undefined

110. _____ of calculus is the statement that the two central operations of calculus, differentiation and integration, are inverse operations: if a continuous function is first integrated and then differentiated, the original function is retrieved.
   a. Thing
   b. Fundamental Theorem of Calculus0
   c. Undefined
   d. Undefined

111. The word _____ is used in a variety of ways in mathematics.
   a. Thing
   b. Index0
   c. Undefined
   d. Undefined

112. In mathematics, especially in order theory, an _____ of a subset S of some partially ordered set is an element of P which is greater than or equal to every element of S.
   a. Thing
   b. Upper bound0
   c. Undefined
   d. Undefined

113. The term _____ refers to the largest and the smallest element of a set.
   a. Extreme value0
   b. Thing
   c. Undefined
   d. Undefined

114. In mathematics, an _____ is a statement about the relative size or order of two objects.

Chapter 7. Techniques of Integration

a. Inequality0
b. Thing
c. Undefined
d. Undefined

115. Generally, a _____ is a splitting of something into parts.
    a. Partition0
    b. Thing
    c. Undefined
    d. Undefined

116. In the mathematical field of numerical analysis, the _____ in some data is the discrepancy between an exact value and some approximation to it.
    a. Approximation Error0
    b. Thing
    c. Undefined
    d. Undefined

117. In Euclidean geometry, an _____ is a closed segment of a differentiable curve in the two-dimensional plane; for example, a circular _____ is a segment of a circle.
    a. Arc0
    b. Concept
    c. Undefined
    d. Undefined

118. _____ also called rectification of a curve—was historically difficult.
    a. Thing
    b. Arc length0
    c. Undefined
    d. Undefined

119. An _____ is the limit of a definite integral, as an endpoint of the interval of integration approaches either a specified real number or ‡ or − ‡ or, in some cases, as both endpoints approach limits.
    a. Thing
    b. Improper integral0
    c. Undefined
    d. Undefined

120. _____ is the state of being greater than any finite real or natural number, however large.
    a. Infinite0
    b. Thing
    c. Undefined
    d. Undefined

121. In mathematics, a set is called _____ if there is a bijection between the set and some set of the form {1, 2, ..., n} where n is a natural number.
    a. Finite0
    b. Thing
    c. Undefined
    d. Undefined

122. Continuous functions are of utmost importance in mathematics and applications. However, not all functions are continuous. If a function is not continuous at a point in its domain, one says that it has a _____ there. The set of all points of _____ of a function may be a discrete set, a dense set, or even the entire domain of the function.
    a. Thing
    b. Discontinuity0
    c. Undefined
    d. Undefined

123. The _____ of a ring R is defined to be the smallest positive integer n such that $n\,a = 0$, for all a in R.
    a. Characteristic0
    b. Thing
    c. Undefined
    d. Undefined

Chapter 7. Techniques of Integration

124. In mathematics, a _____ may be described informally as a number that can be given by an infinite decimal representation.
- a. Thing
- b. Real number0
- c. Undefined
- d. Undefined

125. _____ denotes the approach toward a definite value, as time goes on; or to a definite point, a common view or opinion, or toward a fixed or equilibrium state.
- a. Thing
- b. Convergence0
- c. Undefined
- d. Undefined

126. _____ is an operator that measures the magnitude of a vector field's source or sink at a given point; the _____ of a vector field is a signed scalar.
- a. Divergence0
- b. Thing
- c. Undefined
- d. Undefined

127. _____ is the state of being greater than any finite number, however large.
- a. Infinity0
- b. Thing
- c. Undefined
- d. Undefined

128. _____ of a probability distribution, random variable, or population or multiset of values is a measure of the spread of its values.
- a. Standard deviation0
- b. Thing
- c. Undefined
- d. Undefined

129. _____ is a measure of difference for interval and ratio variables between the observed value and the mean.
- a. Thing
- b. Deviation0
- c. Undefined
- d. Undefined

130. _____ generally derives from name. A _____ quantity e.g., length, diameter, volume, voltage, value is generally the quantity according to which some item has been named or is generally referred to.
- a. Thing
- b. Nominal0
- c. Undefined
- d. Undefined

131. _____ are economic entities that give rise to future economic benefit and is controlled by the entity as a result of past transaction or other events
- a. Thing
- b. Asset0
- c. Undefined
- d. Undefined

132. _____ is a mathematical science pertaining to the collection, analysis, interpretation or explanation, and presentation of data. It is applicable to a wide variety of academic disciplines, from the physical and social sciences to the humanities.
- a. Statistics0
- b. Thing
- c. Undefined
- d. Undefined

133. In mathematics, the _____ (or modulus) of a real number is its numerical value without regard to its sign.

a. Thing
b. Absolute value0
c. Undefined
d. Undefined

134. _____ are objects, characters, or other concrete representations of ideas, concepts, or other abstractions.
a. Symbols0
b. Thing
c. Undefined
d. Undefined

135. In mathematics, a _____ is an algebraic structure in which addition and multiplication are defined and have properties listed below.
a. Ring0
b. Thing
c. Undefined
d. Undefined

136. _____ is a synonym for information.
a. Data0
b. Thing
c. Undefined
d. Undefined

1. In geometry, a line _____ is a part of a line that is bounded by two end points, and contains every point on the line between its end points.
   a. Concept
   b. Segment0
   c. Undefined
   d. Undefined

2. _____ is a set, with some particular properties and usually some additional structure, such as the operations of addition or multiplication, for instance.
   a. Thing
   b. Space0
   c. Undefined
   d. Undefined

3. A _____ is a part of a line that is bounded by two end points, and contains every point on the line between its end points.
   a. Line segment0
   b. Thing
   c. Undefined
   d. Undefined

4. _____ is the middle point of a line segment.
   a. Thing
   b. Midpoint0
   c. Undefined
   d. Undefined

5. In geometry, the _____ of an object is a point in some sense in the middle of the object.
   a. Thing
   b. Center0
   c. Undefined
   d. Undefined

6. In classical geometry, a _____ of a circle or sphere is any line segment from its center to its boundary. By extension, the _____ of a circle or sphere is the length of any such segment. The _____ is half the diameter. In science and engineering the term _____ of curvature is commonly used as a synonym for _____.
   a. Thing
   b. Radius0
   c. Undefined
   d. Undefined

7. In mathematics, a _____ is the set of all points in three-dimensional space (R^3) which are at distance r from a fixed point of that space, where r is a positive real number called the radius of the _____. The fixed point is called the center or centre, and is not part of the _____ itself.
   a. Thing
   b. Sphere0
   c. Undefined
   d. Undefined

8. In linear algebra, the _____ of an n-by-n square matrix A is defined to be the sum of the elements on the main diagonal of A,
   a. Thing
   b. Trace0
   c. Undefined
   d. Undefined

9. A _____ is a set of numbers that designate location in a given reference system, such as x,y in a planar _____ system or an x,y,z in a three-dimensional _____ system.
   a. Coordinate0
   b. Thing
   c. Undefined
   d. Undefined

10. In mathematics, a _____ is a two-dimensional manifold or surface that is perfectly flat.

Chapter 8. Functions of Several Variables

a. Thing
b. Plane0
c. Undefined
d. Undefined

11. In mathematics and its applications, a _____ is a system for assigning an n-tuple of numbers or scalars to each point in an n-dimensional space.
    a. Coordinate system0
    b. Concept
    c. Undefined
    d. Undefined

12. A _____ is a one-dimensional picture in which the integers are shown as specially-marked points evenly spaced on a line.
    a. Thing
    b. Number line0
    c. Undefined
    d. Undefined

13. In geometry, two lines or planes if one falls on the other in such a way as to create congruent adjacent angles. The term may be used as a noun or adjective. Thus, referring to Figure 1, the line AB is the _____ to CD through the point B.
    a. Thing
    b. Perpendicular0
    c. Undefined
    d. Undefined

14. _____ means of or relating to the French philosopher and mathematician René Descartes.
    a. Cartesian0
    b. Thing
    c. Undefined
    d. Undefined

15. In mathematics, _____ geometry was the traditional name for the geometry of three-dimensional Euclidean space — for practical purposes the kind of space we live in.
    a. Thing
    b. Solid0
    c. Undefined
    d. Undefined

16. _____ is the study of geometry using the principles of algebra. _____ can be explained more simply: it is concerned with defining geometrical shapes in a numerical way and extracting numerical information from that representation.
    a. Thing
    b. Analytic geometry0
    c. Undefined
    d. Undefined

17. An _____ is when two lines intersect somewhere on a plane creating a right angle at intersection
    a. Axes0
    b. Thing
    c. Undefined
    d. Undefined

18. In mathematics, the conjugate _____ or adjoint matrix of an m-by-n matrix A with complex entries is the n-by-m matrix A* obtained from A by taking the transpose and then taking the complex conjugate of each entry.
    a. Thing
    b. Pairs0
    c. Undefined
    d. Undefined

19. In mathematics, _____ are two-dimensional manifolds or surfaces that are perfectly flat.
    a. Thing
    b. Planes0
    c. Undefined
    d. Undefined

20. The _____ of measurement are a globally standardized and modernized form of the metric system.
    a. Thing
    b. Units0
    c. Undefined
    d. Undefined

21. A _____ is a symbolic representation denoting a quantity or expression. It often represents an "unknown" quantity that has the potential to change.
    a. Thing
    b. Variable0
    c. Undefined
    d. Undefined

22. In geometry, an _____ is a point at which a line segment or ray terminates.
    a. Thing
    b. Endpoint0
    c. Undefined
    d. Undefined

23. In geometry, a _____ (Greek words diairo = divide and metro = measure) of a circle is any straight line segment that passes through the centre and whose endpoints are on the circular boundary, or, in more modern usage, the length of such a line segment. When using the word in the more modern sense, one speaks of the _____ rather than a _____, because all diameters of a circle have the same length. This length is twice the radius. The _____ of a circle is also the longest chord that the circle has.
    a. Diameter0
    b. Thing
    c. Undefined
    d. Undefined

24. The mathematical concept of a _____ expresses the intuitive idea of deterministic dependence between two quantities, one of which is viewed as primary and the other as secondary. A _____ then is a way to associate a unique output for each input of a specified type, for example, a real number or an element of a given set.
    a. Function0
    b. Thing
    c. Undefined
    d. Undefined

25. In plane geometry, a _____ is a polygon with four equal sides, four right angles, and parallel opposite sides. In algebra, the _____ of a number is that number multiplied by itself.
    a. Thing
    b. Square0
    c. Undefined
    d. Undefined

26. _____ is a technique used in algebra to solve quadratic equations, in analytic geometry for determining the shapes of graphs, and in calculus for computing integrals, including, but hardly limited to, the integrals that define Laplace transforms. The essential objective is to reduce a quadratic polynomial in a variable in an equation or expression to a squared polynomial of linear order. This can reduce an equation or integral to one that is more easily solved or evaluated.
    a. Thing
    b. Completing the square0
    c. Undefined
    d. Undefined

27. In abstract algebra, _____ consists of sets with binary operations that satisfy certain axioms.
    a. Grouping0
    b. Thing
    c. Undefined
    d. Undefined

28. In mathematics, the _____ of two sets A and B is the set that contains all elements of A that also belong to B (or equivalently, all elements of B that also belong to A), but no other elements.

Chapter 8. Functions of Several Variables

a. Intersection0
b. Thing
c. Undefined
d. Undefined

29. In Euclidean geometry, a _____ is the set of all points in a plane at a fixed distance, called the radius, from a given point, the center.
    a. Circle0
    b. Thing
    c. Undefined
    d. Undefined

30. A _____ is one of the basic shapes of geometry: a polygon with three vertices and three sides which are straight line segments.
    a. Triangle0
    b. Thing
    c. Undefined
    d. Undefined

31. In geometry, a _____ is a special kind of point, usually a corner of a polygon, polyhedron, or higher dimensional polytope. In the geometry of curves a _____ is a point of where the first derivative of curvature is zero. In graph theory, a _____ is the fundamental unit out of which graphs are formed
    a. Vertex0
    b. Thing
    c. Undefined
    d. Undefined

32. _____ has one 90° internal angle a right angle.
    a. Thing
    b. Right triangle0
    c. Undefined
    d. Undefined

33. An _____ triange is a triangle with at least two sides of equal length.
    a. Isosceles0
    b. Thing
    c. Undefined
    d. Undefined

34. _____ is a notation for writing numbers that is often used by scientists and mathematicians to make it easier to write large and small numbers.
    a. Thing
    b. Scientific notation0
    c. Undefined
    d. Undefined

35. In trigonometry, the _____ is a function defined as $\tan x = \sin x / \cos x$. The function is so-named because it can be defined as the length of a certain segment of a _____ (in the geometric sense) to the unit circle. In plane geometry, a line is _____ to a curve, at some point, if both line and curve pass through the point with the same direction
    a. Tangent0
    b. Thing
    c. Undefined
    d. Undefined

36. _____ means "constancy", i.e. if something retains a certain feature even after we change a way of looking at it, then it is symmetric.
    a. Thing
    b. Symmetry0
    c. Undefined
    d. Undefined

37. A _____ is a three-dimensional solid object bounded by six square faces, facets, or sides, with three meeting at each vertex.

a. Cube0
b. Thing
c. Undefined
d. Undefined

38. _____ are of a number n in its third power-the result of multiplying it by itself three times.
   a. Cubes0
   b. Thing
   c. Undefined
   d. Undefined

39. A _____ is a unit of length, usually used to measure distance, in a number of different systems, including Imperial units, United States customary units and Norwegian/Swedish mil. Its size can vary from system to system, but in each is between 1 and 10 kilometers. In contemporary English contexts _____ refers to either:
   a. Mile0
   b. Thing
   c. Undefined
   d. Undefined

40. Any point where a graph makes contact with an coordinate axis is called an _____ of the graph
   a. Thing
   b. Intercept0
   c. Undefined
   d. Undefined

41. In mathematics, the _____ of a coordinate system is the point where the axes of the system intersect.
   a. Thing
   b. Origin0
   c. Undefined
   d. Undefined

42. An _____ is a straight line around which a geometric figure can be rotated.
   a. Axis0
   b. Thing
   c. Undefined
   d. Undefined

43. An _____ is a type of quadric surface that is a higher dimensional analogue of an ellipse.
   a. Ellipsoid0
   b. Thing
   c. Undefined
   d. Undefined

44. _____ are the basic objects of study in graph theory. Informally speaking, a graph is a set of objects called points, nodes, or vertices connected by links called lines or edges.
   a. Graphs0
   b. Thing
   c. Undefined
   d. Undefined

45. In mathematics, a _____ is a constant multiplicative factor of a certain object. The object can be such things as a variable, a vector, a function, etc. For example, the _____ of $9x^2$ is 9.
   a. Thing
   b. Coefficient0
   c. Undefined
   d. Undefined

46. Regrouping is the act of putting ones into groups of 10. For example, the 1 on the far right of 131 would be denoted _____ if the digit of the number being subtracted is larger than 1, such as 131-99.
   a. Thing
   b. By 100
   c. Undefined
   d. Undefined

47. A _____ is a three-dimensional geometric shape formed by straight lines through a fixed point (vertex) to the points of a fixed curve (directrix)

Chapter 8. Functions of Several Variables

a. Concept
c. Undefined
b. Cone0
d. Undefined

48. In geometry, _____ lines are two lines that share one or more common points.
    a. Intersecting0
    b. Thing
    c. Undefined
    d. Undefined

49. _____ is a quadric
    a. Thing
    b. Paraboloid0
    c. Undefined
    d. Undefined

50. _____ has many meanings, most of which simply .
    a. Thing
    b. Power0
    c. Undefined
    d. Undefined

51. In mathamatics, a _____ is a quadric, a type of surface in three dimensions, described by the equation
    a. Hyperboloid0
    b. Thing
    c. Undefined
    d. Undefined

52. In mathematics, there are several meanings of _____ depending on the subject.
    a. Thing
    b. Degree0
    c. Undefined
    d. Undefined

53. In mathematics, an _____ .
    a. Thing
    b. Ellipse0
    c. Undefined
    d. Undefined

54. _____ is a quadric, a type of surface in three dimensions
    a. Thing
    b. Elliptic paraboloid0
    c. Undefined
    d. Undefined

55. An _____ is a combination of numbers, operators, grouping symbols and/or free variables and bound variables arranged in a meaningful way which can be evaluated..
    a. Expression0
    b. Thing
    c. Undefined
    d. Undefined

56. In mathematics and the mathematical sciences, a _____ is a fixed, but possibly unspecified, value. This is in contrast to a variable, which is not fixed.
    a. Constant0
    b. Thing
    c. Undefined
    d. Undefined

57. A _____ is a movement of an object in a circular motion. A two-dimensional object rotates around a center (or point) of _____. A three-dimensional object rotates around a line called an axis. If the axis of _____ is within the body, the body is said to rotate upon itself, or spinâ€"which implies relative speed and perhaps free-movement with angular momentum. A circular motion about an external point, e.g. the Earth about the Sun, is called an orbit or more properly an orbital revolution.

Chapter 8. Functions of Several Variables

a. Rotation0
b. Thing
c. Undefined
d. Undefined

58. In physics, _____ is an influence that may cause an object to accelerate. It may be experienced as a lift, a push, or a pull. The actual acceleration of the body is determined by the vector sum of all forces acting on it, known as net _____ or resultant _____.
    a. Force0
    b. Thing
    c. Undefined
    d. Undefined

59. In functional analysis and related areas of mathematics the _____ set of a given subset of a vector space is a certain set in the dual space.
    a. Thing
    b. Polar0
    c. Undefined
    d. Undefined

60. The _____ is an imaginary line on the Earth's surface equidistant from the North Pole and South Pole.
    a. Equator0
    b. Thing
    c. Undefined
    d. Undefined

61. In mathematics, the _____ of a function is the set of all "output" values produced by that function. Given a function $f : A \to B$, the _____ of f, is defined to be the set $\{x \in B : x = f(a) \text{ for some } a \in A\}$.
    a. Range0
    b. Thing
    c. Undefined
    d. Undefined

62. In mathematics, a _____ of a k-place relation $L \subseteq X_1 \times \ldots \times X_k$ is one of the sets X_j, $1 \leq j \leq k$. In the special case where k = 2 and $L \subseteq X_1 \times X_2$ is a function $L : X_1 \to X_2$, it is conventional to refer to X_1 as the _____ of the function and to refer to X_2 as the codomain of the function.
    a. Domain0
    b. Thing
    c. Undefined
    d. Undefined

63. A _____ is a map illustrated with contour lines, for example a topographic map.
    a. Contour map0
    b. Thing
    c. Undefined
    d. Undefined

64. In mathematics, the concept of a _____ tries to capture the intuitive idea of a geometrical one-dimensional and continuous object. A simple example is the circle.
    a. Curve0
    b. Thing
    c. Undefined
    d. Undefined

65. In mathematics, _____ are the intuitive idea of a geometrical one-dimensional and continuous object.
    a. Thing
    b. Curves0
    c. Undefined
    d. Undefined

66. A _____, is a symbolized depiction of space which highlights relations between components of that space. Most usually a _____ is a two-dimensional, geometrically accurate representation of a three-dimensional space.

Chapter 8. Functions of Several Variables

a. Thing
b. Map0
c. Undefined
d. Undefined

67. Mathematical _____ is used to represent ideas.
a. Thing
b. Notation0
c. Undefined
d. Undefined

68. In mathematics, a _____ may be described informally as a number that can be given by an infinite decimal representation.
a. Real number0
b. Thing
c. Undefined
d. Undefined

69. An _____ is a collection of two not necessarily distinct objects, one of which is distinguished as the first coordinate and the other as the second coordinate.
a. Thing
b. Ordered pair0
c. Undefined
d. Undefined

70. The _____ integers are all the integers from zero on upwards.
a. Thing
b. Nonnegative0
c. Undefined
d. Undefined

71. _____ is the symbold used to indicate the nth root of a number
a. Radical0
b. Thing
c. Undefined
d. Undefined

72. In mathematics, the _____ f is the collection of all ordered pairs . In particular, graph means the graphical representation of this collection, in the form of a curve or surface, together with axes, etc. Graphing on a Cartesian plane is sometimes referred to as curve sketching.
a. Graph of a function0
b. Thing
c. Undefined
d. Undefined

73. In mathematics, a _____ is any one of several different types of functions, mappings, operations, or transformations.
a. Thing
b. Projection0
c. Undefined
d. Undefined

74. _____ is electromagnetic radiation with a wavelength that is visible to the eye (visible _____) or, in a technical or scientific context, electromagnetic radiation of any wavelength.
a. Thing
b. Light0
c. Undefined
d. Undefined

75. _____ is the application of tools and a processing medium to the transformation of raw materials into finished goods for sale.
a. Manufacturing0
b. Thing
c. Undefined
d. Undefined

Chapter 8. Functions of Several Variables

76. _____ asserts that the maximum output of a technologically-determined production process is a mathematical function of input factors of production.
    a. Thing
    b. Production function0
    c. Undefined
    d. Undefined

77. _____ is a kind of property which exists as magnitude or multitude. It is among the basic classes of things along with quality, substance, change, and relation.
    a. Amount0
    b. Thing
    c. Undefined
    d. Undefined

78. The _____ of a ring R is defined to be the smallest positive integer n such that n a = 0, for all a in R.
    a. Characteristic0
    b. Thing
    c. Undefined
    d. Undefined

79. A _____ is a method of using property as security for the payment of a debt.
    a. Mortgage0
    b. Thing
    c. Undefined
    d. Undefined

80. A _____ is a special kind of ratio, indicating a relationship between two measurements with different units, such as miles to gallons or cents to pounds.
    a. Thing
    b. Rate0
    c. Undefined
    d. Undefined

81. A _____ is a type of debt. All material things can be lent but this article focuses exclusively on monetary loans. Like all debt instruments, a _____ entails the redistribution of financial assets over time, between the lender and the borrower.
    a. Loan0
    b. Thing
    c. Undefined
    d. Undefined

82. An _____ is an increase, either of some fixed amount, for example added regularly, or of a variable amount.
    a. Increment0
    b. Thing
    c. Undefined
    d. Undefined

83. _____ is the fee paid on borrowed money.
    a. Interest0
    b. Thing
    c. Undefined
    d. Undefined

84. An _____ is the fee paid on borrow money.
    a. Concept
    b. Interest rate0
    c. Undefined
    d. Undefined

85. In mathematics, a _____ number (or a _____) is a natural number that has exactly two (distinct) natural number divisors, which are 1 and the _____ number itself.
    a. Prime0
    b. Thing
    c. Undefined
    d. Undefined

Chapter 8. Functions of Several Variables

86. _____ is the art, science, and practice of studying and managing forests and plantations, and related natural resources.
   a. Thing
   b. Forestry0
   c. Undefined
   d. Undefined

87. In mathematics, a _____ is the result of multiplying, or an expression that identifies factors to be multiplied.
   a. Product0
   b. Thing
   c. Undefined
   d. Undefined

88. _____, from Latin meaning "to make progress", is defined in two different ways. Pure economic _____ is the increase in wealth that an investor has from making an investment, taking into consideration all costs associated with that investment including the opportunity cost of capital.
   a. Profit0
   b. Thing
   c. Undefined
   d. Undefined

89. A _____ is an individual or household that purchases and uses goods and services generated within the economy.
   a. Consumer0
   b. Thing
   c. Undefined
   d. Undefined

90. _____ consists of the knowledge of various products to protect the public from fraudulent or unforseeable circumstances.
   a. Consumer awareness0
   b. Thing
   c. Undefined
   d. Undefined

91. In mathematics, an _____, mean, or central tendency of a data set refers to a measure of the "middle" or "expected" value of the data set.
   a. Concept
   b. Average0
   c. Undefined
   d. Undefined

92. _____ finance, in finance, a debt security, issued by Issuer
   a. Thing
   b. Bond0
   c. Undefined
   d. Undefined

93. _____ or investing is a term with several closely-related meanings in business management, finance and economics, related to saving or deferring consumption.
   a. Investment0
   b. Thing
   c. Undefined
   d. Undefined

94. _____ of an object is its speed in a particular direction.
   a. Velocity0
   b. Thing
   c. Undefined
   d. Undefined

95. _____ of a function of several variables is its derivative with respect to one of those variables with the others held constant as opposed to the total derivative, in which all variables are allowed to vary.

Chapter 8. Functions of Several Variables

a. Partial derivative0
b. Thing
c. Undefined
d. Undefined

96. The _____ is a measurement of how a function changes when the values of its inputs change.
a. Derivative0
b. Thing
c. Undefined
d. Undefined

97. _____ is often used to describe the measurement of the steepness, incline, gradient, or grade of a straight line. The _____ is defined as the ratio of the "rise" divided by the "run" between two points on a line, or in other words, the ratio of the altitude change to the horizontal distance between any two points on the line.
a. Thing
b. Slope0
c. Undefined
d. Undefined

98. In mathematics, an _____ is any of the arguments, i.e. "inputs", to a function. Thus if we have a function f(x), then x is a _____.
a. Independent variable0
b. Thing
c. Undefined
d. Undefined

99. The _____ governs the differentiation of products of differentiable functions.
a. Thing
b. Product rule0
c. Undefined
d. Undefined

100. _____, a field in mathematics, is the study of how functions change when their inputs change. The primary object of study in _____ is the derivative.
a. Thing
b. Differential calculus0
c. Undefined
d. Undefined

101. A _____ of a number is the product of that number with any integer.
a. Multiple0
b. Thing
c. Undefined
d. Undefined

102. _____ has two distinct but etymologically-related meanings: one in geometry and one in trigonometry.
a. Thing
b. Tangent line0
c. Undefined
d. Undefined

103. A pair of angles are _____ if the sum of their angles is 90°.
a. Complementary0
b. Concept
c. Undefined
d. Undefined

104. In economics, supply and _____ describe market relations between prospective sellers and buyers of a good.
a. Thing
b. Demand0
c. Undefined
d. Undefined

105. A _____ is a landform that extends above the surrounding terrain in a limited area. A _____ is generally steeper than a hill, but there is no universally accepted standard definition for the height of a _____ or a hill although a _____ usually has an identifiable summit.

Chapter 8. Functions of Several Variables

    a. Thing
    b. Mountain0
    c. Undefined
    d. Undefined

106. _____ is the change in total cost that arises when the quantity produced changes by one unit.
    a. Marginal cost0
    b. Thing
    c. Undefined
    d. Undefined

107. _____ is the extra revenue that an additional unit of product will bring a firm. It can also be described as the change in total revenue/change in number of units sold.
    a. Thing
    b. Marginal revenue0
    c. Undefined
    d. Undefined

108. _____ is a business term for the amount of money that a company receives from its activities in a given period, mostly from sales of products and/or services to customers
    a. Revenue0
    b. Thing
    c. Undefined
    d. Undefined

109. Acid _____ ratio measures the ability of a company to use its near cash or quick assets to immediately extinguish its current liabilities.
    a. Thing
    b. Test0
    c. Undefined
    d. Undefined

110. _____ is a physical property of a system that underlies the common notions of hot and cold; something that is hotter has the greater _____.
    a. Temperature0
    b. Thing
    c. Undefined
    d. Undefined

111. The metre (or _____, see spelling differences) is a measure of length. It is the basic unit of length in the metric system and in the International System of Units (SI), used around the world for general and scientific purposes.
    a. Concept
    b. Meter0
    c. Undefined
    d. Undefined

112. The word _____ is used in a variety of ways in mathematics.
    a. Index0
    b. Thing
    c. Undefined
    d. Undefined

113. A _____ is a function that assigns a number to subsets of a given set.
    a. Thing
    b. Measure0
    c. Undefined
    d. Undefined

114. _____ is a state in the southern region of the United States of America and was one of the original Thirteen Colonies that revolted against British rule in the American Revolution.
    a. Georgia0
    b. Thing
    c. Undefined
    d. Undefined

115. _____ is a way of expressing a number as a fraction of 100 per cent meaning "per hundred".

Chapter 8. Functions of Several Variables

   a. Thing
   c. Undefined
   b. Percent0
   d. Undefined

116. A frame of _____ is a particular perspective from which the universe is observed.
   a. Reference0
   c. Undefined
   b. Thing
   d. Undefined

117. in mathematics, maxima and minima, known collectively as _____, are the largest value maximum or smallest value minimum, that a function takes in a point either within a given neighborhood or on the function domain in its entirety global extremum.
   a. Thing
   c. Undefined
   b. Extrema0
   d. Undefined

118. The _____ is the highest point in a certain portion of a graph.
   a. Relative maximum0
   c. Undefined
   b. Thing
   d. Undefined

119. The term _____ refers to the largest and the smallest element of a set.
   a. Thing
   c. Undefined
   b. Extreme value0
   d. Undefined

120. _____ is a free computer algebra system based on a 1982 version of Macsyma
   a. Maxima0
   c. Undefined
   b. Thing
   d. Undefined

121. _____ is a mathematical subject that includes the study of limits, derivatives, integrals, and power series and constitutes a major part of modern university curriculum.
   a. Thing
   c. Undefined
   b. Calculus0
   d. Undefined

122. In mathematics, maxima and _____, known collectively as extrema, are points in the domain of a function at which the function takes a largest value .
   a. Thing
   c. Undefined
   b. Minima0
   d. Undefined

123. In mathematics, an inequality is a statement about the relative size or order of two objects. For example 14 > 10, or 14 is _____ 10.
   a. Greater than0
   c. Undefined
   b. Thing
   d. Undefined

124. The _____ is the lowest point in a certain portion of a graph.
   a. Thing
   c. Undefined
   b. Relative minimum0
   d. Undefined

125. In mathematics, defined and _____ are used to explain whether or not expressions have meaningful, sensible, and unambiguous values.

Chapter 8. Functions of Several Variables

    a. Thing
    c. Undefined
    b. Undefined0
    d. Undefined

126. _____ is a point on the domain of a function
    a. Thing
    c. Undefined
    b. Critical point0
    d. Undefined

127. In the most general terms, a _____ for a smooth function (curve, surface or hypersurface) is a point such that the curve/surface/etc. in the neighborhood of this point lies on different sides of the tangent at this point. In certain contexts the definition may vary. It is most frequently used at critical points.
    a. Saddle point0
    c. Undefined
    b. Thing
    d. Undefined

128. _____ the expected value of a random variable displays the average or central value of the variable. It is a summary value of the distribution of the variable.
    a. Thing
    c. Undefined
    b. Determining0
    d. Undefined

129. A _____ function is a function for which, intuitively, small changes in the input result in small changes in the output.
    a. Event
    c. Undefined
    b. Continuous0
    d. Undefined

130. In a mathematical proof or a syllogism, a _____ is a statement that is the logical consequence of preceding statements.
    a. Concept
    c. Undefined
    b. Conclusion0
    d. Undefined

131. The _____ of a solid object is the three-dimensional concept of how much space it occupies, often quantified numerically.
    a. Thing
    c. Undefined
    b. Volume0
    d. Undefined

132. _____ are cubes in which all sides are of the same length and all face perpendicular to each other including an atom at each corner of the unigt cell.
    a. Cubic units0
    c. Undefined
    b. Thing
    d. Undefined

133. In mathematics, the additive inverse, or _____ of a number n is the number that, when added to n, yields zero. The additive inverse of n is denoted −n. For example, 7 is −7, because 7 + (−7) = 0, and the additive inverse of −0.3 is 0.3, because −0.3 + 0.3 = 0.
    a. Opposite0
    c. Undefined
    b. Thing
    d. Undefined

134. In mathematics, the _____ of a number n is the number that, when added to n, yields zero. The _____ of n is denoted −n. For example, 7 is −7, because 7 + (−7) = 0, and the _____ of −0.3 is 0.3, because −0.3 + 0.3 = 0.

a. Thing
b. Additive inverse0
c. Undefined
d. Undefined

135. A _____ is the result of the addition of a set of numbers. The numbers may be natural numbers, complex numbers, matrices, or still more complicated objects. An infinite _____ is a subtle procedure known as a series.
a. Sum0
b. Thing
c. Undefined
d. Undefined

136. _____ are a method for finding the extrema of a function of several variables subject to one or more constraints: it is the basic tool in nonlinear constrained optimization.
a. Thing
b. Lagrange multipliers0
c. Undefined
d. Undefined

137. In mathematics, a _____ is a condition that a solution to an optimization problem must satisfy in order to be acceptable.
a. Thing
b. Constraint0
c. Undefined
d. Undefined

138. In computer science, an _____ is the problem of finding the best solution from all feasible solutions.
a. Thing
b. Optimization problem0
c. Undefined
d. Undefined

139. In mathematics, computing, linguistics, and related disciplines, an _____ is a finite list of well-defined instructions for accomplishing some task which, given an initial state, will terminate in a defined end-state.
a. Concept
b. Algorithm0
c. Undefined
d. Undefined

140. The word _____ comes from the Latin word linearis, which means created by lines.
a. Thing
b. Linear0
c. Undefined
d. Undefined

141. A _____ is an equation in which each term is either a constant or the product of a constant times the first power of a variable.
a. Linear equation0
b. Thing
c. Undefined
d. Undefined

142. In mathematics, maxima and minima, known collectively as extrema, are the largest value maximum or smallest value minimum, that a function takes in a point either within a given neighborhood local _____ or on the function domain in its entirety global _____.
a. Thing
b. Extremum0
c. Undefined
d. Undefined

143. _____ is a special mathematical relationship between two quantities.Two quantities are called proportional if they vary in such a way that one of the quantities is a constant multiple of the other, or equivalently if they have a constant ratio.

Chapter 8. Functions of Several Variables

    a. Thing
    b. Proportionality0
    c. Undefined
    d. Undefined

144. In geometry, _____ angles are angles that have a common ray coming out of the vertex going between two other rays.
    a. Concept
    b. Adjacent0
    c. Undefined
    d. Undefined

145. Compass and straightedge or ruler-and-compass _____ is the _____ of lengths or angles using only an idealized ruler and compass.
    a. Construction0
    b. Thing
    c. Undefined
    d. Undefined

146. In geometry, a _____ is defined as a quadrilateral where all four of its angles are right angles.
    a. Rectangle0
    b. Thing
    c. Undefined
    d. Undefined

147. _____ is the distance around a given two-dimensional object. As a general rule, the _____ of a polygon can always be calculated by adding all the length of the sides together. So, the formula for triangles is P = a + b + c, where a, b and c stand for each side of it. For quadrilaterals the equation is P = a + b + c + d. For equilateral polygons, P = na, where n is the number of sides and a is the side length.
    a. Perimeter0
    b. Thing
    c. Undefined
    d. Undefined

148. _____ is a payment made by a company to its shareholders
    a. Dividend0
    b. Thing
    c. Undefined
    d. Undefined

149. _____ is a synonym for information.
    a. Data0
    b. Thing
    c. Undefined
    d. Undefined

150. A _____ is an abstract model that uses mathematical language to describe the behavior of a system. Eykhoff defined a _____ as 'a representation of the essential aspects of an existing system which presents knowledge of that system in usable form'.
    a. Thing
    b. Mathematical model0
    c. Undefined
    d. Undefined

151. In regression analysis, _____, also known as ordinary _____ analysis is a method for linear regression that determines the values of unknown quantities in a statistical model by minimizing the sum of the residuals difference between the predicted and observed values squared.
    a. Least squares0
    b. Thing
    c. Undefined
    d. Undefined

152. In mathematics, a _____ is a countable collection of open covers of a topological space that satisfies certain separation axioms.

Chapter 8. Functions of Several Variables

a. Thing
b. Development0
c. Undefined
d. Undefined

153. _____ is an approximation of a general function using a linear function more precisely, an affine function.
a. Thing
b. Linear approximation0
c. Undefined
d. Undefined

154. A _____ is a compensation which workers receive in exchange for their labor.
a. Wage0
b. Thing
c. Undefined
d. Undefined

155. In mathematics, _____ growth occurs when the growth rate of a function is always proportional to the function's current size.
a. Exponential0
b. Thing
c. Undefined
d. Undefined

156. _____ is the production of food, feed, fiber, fuel and other goods by the systematic raizing of plants and animals.
a. Thing
b. Agriculture0
c. Undefined
d. Undefined

157. In sociology and biology a _____ is the collection of people or organisms of a particular species living in a given geographic area or space, usually measured by a census.
a. Thing
b. Population0
c. Undefined
d. Undefined

158. _____ is change in population over time, and can be quantified as the change in the number of individuals in a population per unit time.
a. Thing
b. Population growth0
c. Undefined
d. Undefined

159. _____ is the general term that is used to describe physical artifacts of a technology.
a. Hardware0
b. Thing
c. Undefined
d. Undefined

160. The _____ is the total number of human beings alive on the planet Earth at a given time.
a. World population0
b. Thing
c. Undefined
d. Undefined

161. The _____ of a function is an extension of the concept of a sum, and are identified or found through the use of integration.
a. Thing
b. Integral0
c. Undefined
d. Undefined

162. _____ is an extension of the concept of a sum.

Chapter 8. Functions of Several Variables

a. Definite integral0
b. Thing
c. Undefined
d. Undefined

163. In mathematics, a _____ is a statement that can be proved on the basis of explicitly stated or previously agreed assumptions.
a. Theorem0
b. Thing
c. Undefined
d. Undefined

164. In number theory, the _____ of arithmetic (or unique factorization theorem) states that every natural number greater than 1 can be written as a unique product of prime numbers.
a. Concept
b. Fundamental theorem0
c. Undefined
d. Undefined

165. _____ of calculus is the statement that the two central operations of calculus, differentiation and integration, are inverse operations: if a continuous function is first integrated and then differentiated, the original function is retrieved.
a. Fundamental Theorem of Calculus0
b. Thing
c. Undefined
d. Undefined

166. _____ is a process of combining or accumulating. It may also refer to:
a. Thing
b. Integration0
c. Undefined
d. Undefined

167. In calculus, the indefinite integral of a given function i.e. the set of all antiderivatives of the function is always written with a constant, the _____.
a. Constant of integration0
b. Thing
c. Undefined
d. Undefined

168. _____ is a function that extends the concept of an ordinary sum
a. Thing
b. Integrand0
c. Undefined
d. Undefined

169. In mathematics, an _____ on a real vector space is a choice of which ordered bases are "positively" oriented, or right-handed, and which are "negatively" oriented, or left-handed.
a. Thing
b. Orientation0
c. Undefined
d. Undefined

170. In astronomy, geography, geometry and related sciences and contexts, a plane is said to be _____ at a given point if it is locally perpendicular to the gradient of the gravity field, i.e., with the direction of the gravitational force at that point.
a. Horizontal0
b. Thing
c. Undefined
d. Undefined

171. In mathematical analysis and related areas of mathematics, a set is called _____, if it is, in a certain sense, of finite size.
a. Bounded0
b. Thing
c. Undefined
d. Undefined

Chapter 8. Functions of Several Variables

172. In common philosophical language, a proposition or _____, is the content of an assertion, that is, it is true-or-false and defined by the meaning of a particular piece of language.
    a. Concept
    b. Statement0
    c. Undefined
    d. Undefined

173. An _____ is one of eight divisions.
    a. Octant0
    b. Thing
    c. Undefined
    d. Undefined

174. An _____ of a function f is a function F whose derivative is equal to f, i.e., F' = f.
    a. Thing
    b. Antiderivative0
    c. Undefined
    d. Undefined

175. _____ is mass m per unit volume V.
    a. Thing
    b. Density0
    c. Undefined
    d. Undefined

176. In mathematics, factorization (British English: factorisation) or factoring is the decomposition of an object (for example, a number, a polynomial, or a matrix) into a product of other objects, or _____, which when multiplied together give the original.
    a. Factors0
    b. Thing
    c. Undefined
    d. Undefined

177. _____ systems represent systems whose behavior is not expressible as a sum of the behaviors of its descriptors.
    a. Nonlinear0
    b. Thing
    c. Undefined
    d. Undefined

178. A _____ represents a system whose behavior is not expressible as a sum of the behaviors of its descriptors.
    a. Nonlinear system0
    b. Thing
    c. Undefined
    d. Undefined

179. _____ is a branch of mathematics concerning the study of structure, relation and quantity.
    a. Algebra0
    b. Concept
    c. Undefined
    d. Undefined

180. In combinatorial mathematics, a _____ is an un-ordered collection of unique elements.
    a. Concept
    b. Combination0
    c. Undefined
    d. Undefined

181. The _____ of a geographic location is its height above a fixed reference point, often the mean sea level.
    a. Thing
    b. Elevation0
    c. Undefined
    d. Undefined

ANSWER KEY

Chapter 1

1. b	2. b	3. b	4. a	5. b	6. a	7. b	8. b	9. b	10. b
11. b	12. a	13. b	14. a	15. b	16. b	17. a	18. b	19. a	20. b
21. a	22. a	23. b	24. b	25. a	26. a	27. b	28. a	29. a	30. a
31. a	32. a	33. a	34. b	35. a	36. b	37. a	38. b	39. a	40. a
41. b	42. b	43. a	44. a	45. b	46. a	47. b	48. a	49. b	50. a
51. a	52. b	53. a	54. a	55. a	56. a	57. a	58. a	59. b	60. b
61. a	62. b	63. b	64. b	65. a	66. b	67. a	68. b	69. b	70. b
71. b	72. a	73. b	74. a	75. a	76. b	77. b	78. b	79. a	80. b
81. b	82. a	83. b	84. a	85. a	86. a	87. a	88. a	89. b	90. a
91. a	92. a	93. b	94. a	95. b	96. a	97. b	98. b	99. b	100. a
101. a	102. b	103. a	104. a	105. a	106. b	107. a	108. a	109. b	110. a
111. b	112. b								

Chapter 2

1. a	2. a	3. b	4. b	5. a	6. b	7. b	8. a	9. a	10. b
11. b	12. a	13. b	14. a	15. a	16. a	17. b	18. a	19. a	20. a
21. b	22. b	23. a	24. b	25. a	26. a	27. b	28. a	29. a	30. b
31. b	32. a	33. a	34. b	35. a	36. b	37. a	38. a	39. a	40. b
41. a	42. b	43. b	44. b	45. b	46. a	47. b	48. a	49. a	50. b
51. a	52. b	53. a	54. a	55. b	56. a	57. b	58. a	59. a	60. a
61. a	62. b	63. a	64. b	65. a	66. a	67. b	68. b	69. a	70. b
71. b	72. b	73. b	74. b	75. b	76. b	77. a	78. b	79. a	80. a
81. b	82. a	83. a	84. a	85. b	86. b	87. b	88. b	89. b	90. b
91. a	92. b	93. b	94. b	95. b	96. b	97. a	98. a	99. b	100. a
101. a	102. a	103. b	104. b	105. a	106. a	107. a	108. a	109. b	110. a
111. b	112. b	113. a	114. b	115. a	116. a	117. b	118. b	119. a	120. a
121. a	122. b	123. b	124. a	125. b	126. b	127. a	128. a	129. a	130. b
131. a	132. b	133. a	134. b	135. b	136. a	137. b	138. b	139. a	140. b
141. a	142. b	143. b	144. a	145. a	146. b	147. b	148. a	149. a	150. b
151. a	152. b	153. b	154. b	155. b	156. a	157. a	158. b	159. b	160. a
161. a	162. b	163. b	164. a	165. b	166. b	167. b	168. b	169. b	170. a
171. b	172. a	173. b	174. b	175. b	176. b	177. b	178. a	179. b	180. b
181. b	182. a								

Chapter 3

1. a	2. b	3. a	4. b	5. b	6. a	7. a	8. a	9. b	10. b
11. b	12. a	13. a	14. b	15. b	16. a	17. a	18. a	19. a	20. a
21. a	22. a	23. b	24. b	25. b	26. a	27. a	28. a	29. b	30. a
31. b	32. b	33. a	34. b	35. b	36. b	37. a	38. a	39. a	40. b
41. b	42. b	43. b	44. b	45. b	46. b	47. b	48. b	49. a	50. a
51. a	52. b	53. b	54. a	55. b	56. b	57. a	58. a	59. b	60. a
61. b	62. a	63. b	64. a	65. b	66. a	67. b	68. a	69. b	70. a
71. a	72. b	73. a	74. a	75. a	76. b	77. b	78. a	79. b	80. b
81. b	82. a	83. a	84. b	85. b	86. b	87. a	88. a	89. a	90. a
91. a	92. a	93. b	94. a	95. b	96. a	97. a	98. b	99. a	100. a
101. a	102. a	103. b	104. b	105. b	106. a	107. b	108. b	109. a	110. a
111. b	112. a	113. a	114. a	115. b	116. a	117. b	118. b	119. b	120. a
121. a	122. b	123. b	124. a	125. a	126. a	127. b	128. b	129. b	130. b
131. a	132. a	133. b	134. b	135. a	136. b	137. b	138. b	139. a	140. a
141. b	142. a	143. a	144. a	145. b	146. a	147. b	148. b	149. a	150. b
151. b	152. b	153. b	154. b	155. a	156. a	157. b	158. b	159. b	160. b
161. b	162. a	163. a	164. b	165. b	166. a	167. a	168. b	169. a	170. b
171. a	172. b	173. b	174. b	175. b					

Chapter 4

1. a	2. a	3. a	4. a	5. b	6. a	7. b	8. b	9. a	10. b
11. b	12. a	13. a	14. a	15. b	16. b	17. b	18. a	19. b	20. a
21. b	22. a	23. a	24. a	25. b	26. b	27. a	28. a	29. b	30. b
31. b	32. a	33. b	34. a	35. a	36. b	37. a	38. a	39. b	40. a
41. a	42. b	43. a	44. a	45. a	46. b	47. a	48. a	49. b	50. a
51. b	52. b	53. b	54. a	55. b	56. a	57. b	58. b	59. a	60. a
61. b	62. b	63. a	64. b	65. b	66. b	67. a	68. a	69. b	70. b
71. a	72. b	73. b	74. a	75. a	76. a	77. a	78. a	79. b	80. b
81. b	82. a	83. a	84. a	85. a	86. b	87. b	88. a	89. b	90. a
91. a	92. b	93. b	94. a	95. b	96. a	97. a	98. a	99. a	100. b
101. a	102. a	103. b	104. a	105. b	106. b	107. a	108. a	109. b	110. b
111. b	112. b	113. a	114. a	115. a	116. a	117. b	118. b	119. b	120. b
121. b	122. a	123. b	124. a	125. a	126. b	127. b	128. a	129. a	130. b
131. a	132. b	133. a	134. a	135. a	136. a	137. a	138. b	139. a	140. a
141. a	142. a	143. a	144. b	145. b	146. a	147. a	148. b	149. b	150. a
151. a	152. b	153. a	154. a	155. b	156. a				

ANSWER KEY

Chapter 5

1. a	2. a	3. a	4. b	5. b	6. b	7. b	8. b	9. a	10. b
11. b	12. b	13. a	14. b	15. a	16. a	17. a	18. a	19. b	20. a
21. a	22. b	23. a	24. b	25. a	26. a	27. a	28. a	29. a	30. a
31. a	32. a	33. b	34. a	35. b	36. b	37. a	38. b	39. a	40. b
41. b	42. a	43. b	44. b	45. b	46. b	47. a	48. b	49. b	50. b
51. b	52. b	53. a	54. b	55. b	56. b	57. a	58. b	59. b	60. a
61. b	62. a	63. b	64. a	65. b	66. a	67. a	68. a	69. a	70. a
71. b	72. a	73. b	74. a	75. b	76. a	77. b	78. b	79. b	80. a
81. b	82. a	83. b	84. a	85. a	86. a	87. a	88. a	89. b	90. a
91. b	92. b	93. a	94. a	95. b	96. a	97. b	98. b	99. a	100. b
101. a	102. b	103. b	104. b	105. b	106. b	107. b	108. b	109. b	110. a
111. b	112. b	113. a	114. b	115. a	116. b	117. b	118. b	119. a	120. b
121. b	122. b	123. b	124. b	125. b	126. a	127. a	128. b	129. a	130. a
131. b	132. b	133. b	134. b	135. b	136. a	137. a	138. b	139. b	140. a
141. a	142. a	143. b	144. a	145. b	146. a	147. a	148. a	149. a	150. a

Chapter 6

1. a	2. b	3. b	4. a	5. a	6. a	7. a	8. a	9. a	10. b
11. b	12. a	13. a	14. b	15. b	16. a	17. a	18. a	19. b	20. a
21. b	22. a	23. b	24. a	25. b	26. a	27. a	28. a	29. a	30. a
31. b	32. b	33. b	34. a	35. b	36. b	37. b	38. b	39. b	40. b
41. b	42. a	43. b	44. a	45. a	46. a	47. a	48. a	49. b	50. b
51. a	52. b	53. a	54. a	55. a	56. a	57. b	58. a	59. b	60. a
61. b	62. b	63. a	64. a	65. a	66. a	67. b	68. b	69. b	70. b
71. b	72. a	73. a	74. b	75. b	76. b	77. b	78. a	79. b	80. a
81. a	82. a	83. b	84. a	85. a	86. b	87. b	88. b	89. a	90. a
91. a	92. a	93. a	94. a	95. a	96. b	97. b	98. a	99. b	100. b
101. a	102. a	103. b	104. b	105. a	106. b	107. b	108. b	109. b	110. a
111. a	112. b	113. b	114. a	115. a	116. a	117. a	118. a	119. b	120. b
121. a	122. a	123. b	124. a	125. a	126. b	127. b	128. b	129. b	130. a
131. a	132. b	133. a	134. b	135. a	136. a	137. a	138. a	139. b	140. a
141. a	142. b	143. a							

Chapter 7

1. b	2. b	3. b	4. b	5. b	6. a	7. a	8. b	9. a	10. a
11. b	12. a	13. b	14. a	15. b	16. a	17. b	18. a	19. a	20. b
21. a	22. b	23. a	24. b	25. b	26. b	27. a	28. a	29. b	30. b
31. b	32. b	33. b	34. b	35. b	36. b	37. a	38. b	39. a	40. b
41. a	42. b	43. a	44. b	45. a	46. b	47. a	48. a	49. a	50. b
51. a	52. a	53. a	54. b	55. b	56. a	57. a	58. b	59. a	60. a
61. b	62. b	63. b	64. a	65. a	66. a	67. a	68. b	69. a	70. a
71. a	72. a	73. b	74. a	75. a	76. b	77. b	78. b	79. b	80. b
81. b	82. b	83. a	84. b	85. b	86. a	87. a	88. a	89. a	90. a
91. a	92. a	93. b	94. b	95. a	96. b	97. a	98. a	99. a	100. b
101. a	102. a	103. b	104. a	105. a	106. a	107. b	108. a	109. a	110. b
111. b	112. b	113. a	114. a	115. a	116. a	117. a	118. b	119. b	120. a
121. a	122. b	123. a	124. b	125. b	126. a	127. a	128. a	129. b	130. b
131. b	132. a	133. b	134. a	135. a	136. a				

Chapter 8

1. b	2. b	3. a	4. b	5. b	6. b	7. b	8. b	9. a	10. b
11. a	12. b	13. b	14. a	15. b	16. b	17. a	18. b	19. b	20. b
21. b	22. b	23. a	24. a	25. b	26. b	27. a	28. a	29. a	30. a
31. a	32. b	33. a	34. b	35. a	36. b	37. a	38. a	39. a	40. b
41. b	42. a	43. a	44. a	45. b	46. b	47. b	48. a	49. b	50. b
51. a	52. b	53. b	54. b	55. a	56. a	57. a	58. b	59. b	60. a
61. a	62. a	63. a	64. a	65. b	66. b	67. b	68. a	69. b	70. b
71. a	72. a	73. b	74. b	75. a	76. b	77. a	78. a	79. a	80. b
81. a	82. a	83. a	84. b	85. a	86. b	87. a	88. a	89. a	90. a
91. b	92. b	93. a	94. a	95. a	96. a	97. b	98. a	99. b	100. b
101. a	102. b	103. a	104. b	105. b	106. a	107. b	108. a	109. b	110. a
111. b	112. a	113. b	114. a	115. b	116. a	117. b	118. a	119. b	120. a
121. b	122. b	123. a	124. b	125. b	126. b	127. a	128. b	129. b	130. b
131. b	132. a	133. a	134. b	135. a	136. b	137. b	138. b	139. b	140. b
141. a	142. b	143. b	144. b	145. a	146. a	147. a	148. a	149. a	150. b
151. a	152. b	153. b	154. a	155. a	156. b	157. b	158. b	159. a	160. a
161. b	162. a	163. a	164. b	165. a	166. b	167. a	168. b	169. b	170. a
171. a	172. b	173. a	174. b	175. b	176. a	177. a	178. a	179. a	180. b
181. b									

www.ingramcontent.com/pod-product-compliance
Lightning Source LLC
Chambersburg PA
CBHW082042230426
43670CB00016B/2754